T0316603

Cambridge Elements

Elements in the Economics of Emerging Markets
edited by
Bruno S. Sergi
Harvard University

THE PARADOX OF GENDER EQUALITY AND ECONOMIC OUTCOMES IN SUB-SAHARAN AFRICA

The Role of Land Rights

Evelyn F. Wamboye
The Pennsylvania State University

CAMBRIDGE
UNIVERSITY PRESS

Shaftesbury Road, Cambridge CB2 8EA, United Kingdom

One Liberty Plaza, 20th Floor, New York, NY 10006, USA

477 Williamstown Road, Port Melbourne, VIC 3207, Australia

314–321, 3rd Floor, Plot 3, Splendor Forum, Jasola District Centre,
New Delhi – 110025, India

103 Penang Road, #05–06/07, Visioncrest Commercial, Singapore 238467

Cambridge University Press is part of Cambridge University Press & Assessment,
a department of the University of Cambridge.

We share the University's mission to contribute to society through the pursuit of
education, learning and research at the highest international levels of excellence.

www.cambridge.org
Information on this title: www.cambridge.org/9781009371889

DOI: 10.1017/9781009371872

First published 2023

A catalogue record for this publication is available from the British Library

ISBN 978-1-009-37188-9 Paperback
ISSN 2631-8598 (online)
ISSN 2631-858X (print)

Cambridge University Press & Assessment has no responsibility for the persistence
or accuracy of URLs for external or third-party internet websites referred to in this
publication and does not guarantee that any content on such websites is, or will
remain, accurate or appropriate.

The Paradox of Gender Equality and Economic Outcomes in Sub-Saharan Africa

The Role of Land Rights

Elements in the Economics of Emerging Markets

DOI: 10.1017/9781009371872
First published online: September 2023

Evelyn F. Wamboye
The Pennsylvania State University
Author for correspondence: Evelyn F. Wamboye, efw10@psu.edu

Abstract: This Element provides an in-depth analysis of the role of women's ownership of and access to land in sub-Saharan Africa (SSA) in determining gender equality and women's economic and social outcomes and gives suggestions to inform effective gender-sensitive land policies. Using cross-sectional regression analysis, we find that ownership of land by women positively contributes to women's absolute employment. Conversely, results from pairwise correlation show that a lack of ownership of land by women is highly correlated with increased women's unemployment. Despite these findings, the proportion of women who own land in SSA is lower than that of men. Moreover, women usually acquire land through either purchase from the market system or marriage, and even then their rights of ownership are usually very limited and precarious compared to the rights of men.

Keywords: land inheritance, land ownership, land access, gender equality, sub-Saharan Africa

JEL classifications: B54, J16, J21, O55

ISBNs: 9781009371889 (PB), 9781009371872 (OC)
ISSNs: 2631-8598 (online), 2631-858X (print)

Contents

1 Introduction

The process that denies women equal rights compared to men is directly interlinked with the economic and social opportunities that come with those rights and, in aggregate, to a country's economic development, as alluded to in Sen's (1999) book *Development As Freedom*. Indeed, strides have been made in granting women some rights, thanks to the struggle for women's suffrage and numerous other feminist movements as well as the efforts of international organizations that continue to fight for women's social and economic rights and freedoms (Global Fund for Women, 2018; Dancer, 2017; Saiget, 2016). Moreover, many governments now recognize the rights that women have fought for and have taken deliberate measures to protect them (at least in theory) by incorporating the relevant provisions in statutory law (Santos et al., 2014). Some women have benefited from such laws, including the right to vote, but many are still disadvantaged in social (lower educational attainment; lack of empowerment to make decisions impacting their health and well-being and participation in public decision-making) and economic (poor access to formal employment and high-value jobs) outcomes. This is exacerbated by poverty and illiteracy, especially for women in developing countries, where these issues are intertwined and have an inevitable causal relationship with an absence of basic human rights and freedoms (World Bank, 2012). In fact, in many instances, women in sub-Saharan Africa (SSA) are unaware of their legal rights and freedoms beyond what is dictated to them by their clan or tribal norms and customs. And even when laws to protect women's rights exist and women are aware of them, most often many women feel strongly bound by the norms and customs within their groups, which impair or override any statutory laws. Furthermore, institutions that are meant to protect and advance women's rights are predominantly staffed by men whose gender-discriminatory ideologies impair their judgments and decisions.

In this Element, we take a narrow approach and focus on the right of women to own land in SSA as a means to promote gender equality and empower women in the region. The Element is relevant in many ways in terms of both its geographical focus and contribution to the literature and discussions on women's inheritance of land in Africa. A large proportion of the poorest people in the world are in SSA, as evidenced by the disproportionate concentration of the number (thirty-three out of forty-six) of least developed countries (LDCs) in the region (DESA, 2022). In fact, the United Nations estimates that roughly 83.7 percent (2022 estimates) of the world's extremely poor women and girls live in just two regions: SSA (62.8 percent) and Central and South Asia (20.9 percent) (UN Women, 2022). From a global perspective, more than

50 percent of the poor globally tend to be women and girls (51 percent by 2022 estimates), which holds true across age and marital spectra (UN, 2015; UN Women, 2022). In a region where ownership of and access to land determine both economic and social outcomes of individuals and families – and where women are at the heart of the society and at the center of food production – it becomes obvious how land and poverty are intertwined and why women's ownership of and access to land in SSA is an important social and economic policy issue that warrants more study and exploration.

The goal of this Element, therefore, is to provide an in-depth analysis of the role of women's ownership of and access to land in SSA in determining gender equality and women's economic and social outcomes. A number of studies have explored general access to and ownership of land in SSA (Dolcerocca, 2022; Djurfeldt, 2020; Genicot and Hernandez-de-Benito, 2022; Santpoort et al., 2021; Slavchevska et al., 2021), with most of these studies focusing on the marriage channel (Bose and Das, 2017; Cooper, 2012; Doss et al., 2012; Evans, 2015; Evans et al., 2015; FAO, 2008; Jacobs and Kes, 2015; Kalabamu, 2006; Kimani, 2012; Odeny, 2013; UN Women, 2018; Wanyeki, 2012; Yeboah, 2014). Also, a large quantity of this literature is exploratory in nature, probably owing to lack of published household-level data on land ownership and channels through which land is acquired in SSA. A few of these studies have attempted to use anecdotal evidence and/or survey data for individual countries in SSA, but they tend to limit themselves to specific regions within the country. For example, Jacobs and Kes (2015) and Doss et al. (2012) use individual-level survey data for Uganda and South Africa, while Evans et al. (2015) study the connection between tree crops and women's access to and use of land in Ghana. We deviate from these studies and look at the inheritance channel through birthright, with the conviction that, relative to the marriage channel, it is the most effective channel, with no strings attached, and is socially and economically empowering. However, like other scholars, we have to acknowledge the limitations of data in this specific area and therefore hope that this Element (at a minimum) will serve to bring attention to the conversations on women's land inheritance in SSA and spur related empirical research as data becomes available.

Equal rights and proactive protection of the right of women and girls to inherit and own land in SSA is important to the expansion of the capabilities of women and girls to lead the kind of lives they value and have reason to value (Sen, 1999). This can only be achieved when the governments and civil society in the region truly recognize the value and importance of women and girls in the economic, social, and political spheres of individual countries and SSA in general. Moreover, strengthening women's and girls' land rights is an issue that is in alignment with realizing the Sustainable Development Goals (SDGs) 1 and 5 of ending all forms of poverty (Goal 1) and achieving gender equality and empowering all women and girls (Goal 5).

2 Background

Agriculture and rural life are the backbone of African societies. Roughly 62 percent of SSA's population lives in rural communities compared to 36 percent in the Middle East and North Africa (MENA) and 47 percent worldwide (see Table 1). In SSA, the agricultural sector, which is predominantly practiced on small family plots with largely family workers, and which is less mechanized than in many other regions of the world, contributes to approximately 56 percent of total employment in the region, which is more than three times that for MENA (18 percent) and almost twice that globally (30 percent) (see Table 2). Also, a large percentage of farmworkers in SSA tend to be women (57 percent), with men's employment in the sector being about 1 percent lower (see Table 2; see also AUC-ECA-AfDB Consortium, 2010). As mentioned, the majority of agricultural sector labor are family workers. Contributing family workers in SSA account for about 24 percent of total employment (compared to 6 percent in MENA and 12 percent globally), and these family workers are disproportionately women (34 percent), compared to only 16 percent of male employment categorized as contributing family workers (Table 2).

In SSA's small- and medium-sized towns, the informal sector, which depends heavily on land, dominates economic activities, and nine out of ten informal workers are women and youth (AUC, 2011; ECA, 2015). The sector comprises 70 percent of total employment in SSA and roughly 86 percent for Africa in general (ECA, 2015). It is also the single largest contributor to gross domestic

Table 1 Percentage of rural and urban populations (averaged over the years 2007– 2021)

Region	Rural population (% of total population)	Urban population (% of total population)
Middle East and North Africa (MENA)	36.03	63.97
Sub-Saharan Africa (SSA)	61.91	38.09
Worldwide	46.56	53.44

Data source: Author's calculations based on the World Bank's World Development Indicators online database, downloaded on October 21, 2022.

Table 2 Female versus male schooling and employment measures, averaged over the years 2010–2019

Indicator	Middle East and North Africa (MENA)	Sub-Saharan Africa (SSA)	World
Children out of school (% of primary school age)	4.44	18.57	7.66
Children out of school, female (% of female primary school age)	2.40	20.75	8.38
Children out of school, male (% of male primary school age)	1.52	16.44	6.99
Contributing family workers, female (% of female employment) (modeled ILO estimate)	17.87	33.76	19.53
Contributing family workers, male (% of male employment) (modeled ILO estimate)	3.65	15.59	7.05
Contributing family workers, total (% of total employment) (modeled ILO estimate)	6.26	23.95	11.89
Employment in agriculture (% of total employment) (modeled ILO estimate)	17.68	55.95	29.97
Employment in agriculture, female (% of female employment) (modeled ILO estimate)	23.74	56.50	29.20
Employment in agriculture, male (% of male employment) (modeled ILO estimate)	16.32	55.51	30.46

Employment in industry (% of total employment) (modeled ILO estimate)	26.67	10.85	22.93
Employment in industry, female (% of female employment) (modeled ILO estimate)	12.37	7.82	17.25
Employment in industry, male (% of male employment) (modeled ILO estimate)	29.89	13.42	26.53
Employment in services (% of total employment) (modeled ILO estimate)	55.65	33.20	47.10
Employment in services, female (% of female employment) (modeled ILO estimate)	63.90	35.69	53.56
Employment in services, male (% of male employment) (modeled ILO estimate)	53.78	31.07	43.01
Employment to population ratio, 15+, female (%) (modeled ILO estimate)	16.50	57.13	45.38
Employment to population ratio, 15+, male (%) (modeled ILO estimate)	67.86	68.98	71.67
Employment to population ratio, 15+, total (%) (modeled ILO estimate)	43.17	62.97	58.50

Note: ILO (International Labour Organization).

Data source: Author's calculations based on the World Bank's World Development Indicators online database, downloaded on March 27, 2020.

product (GDP) in most SSA countries, valued at 50–80 percent of economic activities in the region (Benjamin et al., 2012; ECA, 2015; Grynberg, 2013). Moreover, evidence shows that most of the informal sector's jobs derive from the agricultural and services sectors, and in countries such as Senegal the share of informal sector in value addition in agriculture and forestry is close to 100 percent (Benjamin et al., 2012; ECA, 2015). As a result, land is an important economic resource, a cornerstone of economic development, and a means of achieving food security and overcoming extreme poverty in the region (Doss et al., 2012; Ellis and Mdoe, 2003; Odeny, 2013; Odgaard, 2002). From an entrepreneurial perspective, land plays a vital role in investment strategies, especially for the small and medium businesses that characterize much of SSA countries' small towns and rural communities. For instance, in order to access financial credit via the formal financial sector, in most countries in SSA land title is required as collateral (Arekapudi and Almodovar-Retegius, 2020). Beyond the economic relevance, land ownership in SSA is a source of social identity and political power, cultural heritage, and insurance for the continuity of clan/family lineage (Arekapudi and Almodovar-Retegius, 2020; Evans, 2016).

The economic, social, and political importance of access to and ownership of land, and the determination of the right to access and ownership, is as old as humankind itself. Kings, monarchs, and other forms of aristocracies (including chiefdoms) were born out of who owned the most hectares of land, which was a measure of wealth and hence political power and socioeconomic status. Participation in governance and membership in decision-making bodies were accorded based on land ownership. The modern-day US government that is celebrated as an example of democracy was based on ownership and access to land. An excerpt from Acemoglu and Robinson's (2012) book *Why Nations Fail* clearly illustrates this point:

> By the 1720s, all the thirteen colonies of what was to become the United States had similar structures of government. In all cases, there was a governor, and an assembly based on a franchise of male property (land) holders. They were not democracies; women, slaves, and the propertyless could not vote. It was these assemblies and their leaders that coalesced to form the First Continental Congress in 1774, the prelude to the independence of the United States. (p. 28)

Women stand to benefit from land ownership in the same way men have for centuries. More importantly, the multiplier effects of the economic and social impact of women's ownership of land are far-reaching compared to those accrued from men as landlords (Afridi, 2010; Duflo, 2003; Jones and Frick,

2010; Rabenhorst, 2011). But, to understand the impact, we must first understand the barriers that have hindered women from owning land.

First and foremost, it is now well documented that women are more likely to face discrimination in land ownership from patrilineal rather than matrilineal land tenure systems. The former arises in patriarchal societies in which a network of social, political, and economic relationships dominated by men control women's labor, reproductive choices, and sexuality, as well as define women's status, privileges, and rights in the society (Kalabamu, 2006). The patriarchal system is reproduced and perpetuated through the ability of fathers (in some cases, with the help of mothers) to bequeath to their sons the power to command resources, direct the labor of their wives and children, and monopolize control of the public sphere, as well as to enforce ideologies that legitimize this system as natural, godly, and unimpeachable (MacInnes, 1998).

Second, society (regardless of geographical location) has effectively socialized women (starting with young girls) to believe that they are in some ways the weaker or inferior gender and are only endowed with reproductive and care capabilities. By implication, the rest of the responsibilities (including resource management) require "masculinity" and thus are beyond the natural abilities of women. But at the heart of all this is the knowledge and fear by men of the empowerment that comes with resource ownership and management. This is a classic form of class struggle, where the class that controls resources becomes the upper or ruling class and the resource-poor class becomes the subjects.

Men's views and fears about women owning land and other productive resources are in many ways clichéd, misconstrued, and unproductive (Lambert et al., 2014). In fact, men and the society at large benefit from women owning land. The same view was held about women receiving an education, which excluded a large percentage of the population from the skilled labor force. Land ownership by women improves their bargaining power and enhances their ability to survive outside of unproductive power structures or gender relationships (Agarwal, 1997; Cooper and Bird, 2012; Deere and Doss, 2006; Evans, 2015). It also empowers women by raising their self-esteem (Hunt and Kasynathan, 2001), social capital (Kabeer, 2001), and physical capital (Evans, 2015). Increased economic and social power implies that women are able to improve their health by negotiating for safer sex, including protection against sexually transmitted diseases (e.g. HIV and AIDS), minimizing the risk of domestic violence (Bhatla et al., 2006; Swaminathan et al., 2008), and having the resources to hedge themselves and their families against pandemics (such as COVID-19) that tend to adversely affect women disproportionately as they necessitate the restriction of the income-generating activities that women depend on. Women are also more likely to improve their earning capacity directly via increased agricultural output and other entrepreneurial activities and indirectly via access to bank credit (Jones and Frick, 2010; Arekapudi and Almodovar-Retegius, 2020). This in turn translates to increased purchasing power for goods and services that improve the welfare of the entire household, such as education, healthcare, and nutrition (Doss, 2006; Duflo, 2003; Jones and Frick, 2010; Katz and Chamorro, 2003; Quisumbing and Mahuccio, 2003). An excerpt from a UN Women (2018) study on securing rural women's access to land in Cameroon clearly illustrates these points:

> In this farmland, I cultivate yams, groundnuts, maize and cassava for home consumption and the excess is sold in the local market and the proceeds used to cater for my family and send the children to school. With the land title, I can easily obtain a loan from the local micro finance institutions to enable me to pay workers to cultivate my farm since I am getting old.

3 Literature Review

Gender inequality in land access and ownership in SSA (Aldasher et al., 2012; Berge et al., 2014; Doss et al., 2012; Jacobs and Kes, 2015) and in other developing regions (Deere, 2017; Deere et al., 2013; Doss et al., 2011) has been widely documented. These studies can be categorized according to two major themes:

(1) The channels through which women acquire and own land.[1]
(2) Women's inheritance and land rights: challenges, opportunities, and household well-being.[2]

While these studies differ in term of geographical coverage, thematic focus, and research methods, there is consensus that women own less land and other immovable assets compared to men and even much lower agricultural land wealth. For example, rates of women land ownership range from 48 percent in Ecuador to 38 percent in Ghana, 32.3 percent in Mexico, 20 percent in India (Karnataka), and 13 percent in Honduras (Deere and León, 2009; Doss et al., 2011; Doss et al., 2012). The rate is even lower for agricultural land wealth, with only 12 percent being held by women in India and 24 percent in Ghana (Doss et al., 2012). Also, evidence from some of the studies (see Doss et al., 2012)

---

[1] See Agarwal (2003); Cooper (2012); Doss et al. (2012); Jacobs and Kes (2015).
[2] See Afridi (2010); Aldasher et al. (2012); Berge et al. (2014); Bose and Das (2017); Dancer (2017); Duflo (2003); Evans (2015, 2016); Evans et al. (2015); Ferrara and Milazzo (2017); Izumi (2007); Joireman (2008); Kelkar (2014); Kumar and Quisumbing (2012); Lambert et al. (2014); Massay (2020); Meinzen-Dick et al. (2019); Mufere (2014); Peterman (2012), World Bank (2012).

demonstrates that women who own land are more likely to have acquired it through, first, purchase (30 percent), then marriage (16 percent), and lastly, inheritance (13 percent).

3.1 Channels through Which Women Acquire and Own Land in SSA

Aside from purchase, there are two major channels through which women can naturally acquire and own land in SSA: inheritance and marriage. While men have secure and legal guarantees to own land through both channels, women's position depends on luck and a number of favorable circumstances, even in the presence of legal protection. In fact, there is an increasing body of literature providing evidence of the insecure position of women's land rights.[3]

Undoubtedly, land is the most valuable resource in SSA and an exclusion of women from land inheritance exacerbates their vulnerability to chronic and intergenerational poverty (Bird, 2007; Doss et al., 2012). Therefore, it is paramount to understand gender patterns in land access and ownership in SSA in order to have a clear grasp of women's social and economic vulnerabilities as well as opportunities in the region (Doss et al., 2012).

3.1.1 The Inheritance Channel

Inheritance is the most important and cheapest channel for acquiring productive assets such as land. As part of a person's birthright, it is the natural and cheapest means through which women can acquire and own land in SSA, and it accords women the same economic opportunities as their male siblings from the start. However, in nearly all SSA countries, patriarchal patterns in land inheritance persist despite these countries' commitment to gender equality goals and national land reforms (Claassens and Ngubane, 2008; Slavchevska et al., 2021; Walker, 2005). In particular, patriarchal laws and traditions effectively characterize land as the property of men and their sons, with women (daughters, sisters, and wives) enjoying secondary access through their male relations (Budlender and Alma, 2011; Claassens and Ngubane, 2008; Errico, 2021; Joireman, 2007; Rugadya, 2010). Arguments that women's ownership of assets such as land would *empower* them, encourage unruly behaviors, and discourage or break up marriages are often used to justify denying land inheritance to women (Kalabamu, 1998). In countries such as Eswatini, women cannot own land under any circumstances because they are considered minors by law

---

[3] See Agarwal (2003); Budlender and Alma (2011); Claasens and Ngubane (2008); Cooper (2012); Doss et al. (2012); Genicot and Hernandez-de-Benito (2022); Jacobs and Kes (2015); Joireman (2007); Rugadya (2010); Slavchevska et al. (2021).

(Kimani, 2012). In Lesotho, women (regardless of age or marital status) are defined as the children of their fathers (when unmarried), husbands (when married), or sons/heirs (when widowed) (Molapo, 1994). However, there are some exceptions such as Comoros (especially on the main island) where only women and girls inherit land, houses, and other assets from their fathers. According to customary traditions in Comoros, a father has a responsibility to build houses for his daughters, and upon marriage husbands move into their wife's home rather than the other way round as it is elsewhere under patriarchal systems in Africa. Overall, women in most countries in SSA are treated as people in transit from their natal to marital homes and are therefore expected to get married if they want to own or access land (FAO, 2008; Odeny, 2013).

International and domestic women rights advocacy groups have taken up the question of land inheritance in Africa on the grounds that it is both a human rights and a socioeconomic issue, particularly in light of the negative impact of HIV and AIDS, the plight of women after divorce or death of a spouse, and human displacement due to civil strife in countries such as Rwanda, Uganda, Democratic Republic of Congo, and Angola as well as forced evictions as a result of foreign direct investment (FDI) in land in places like the Gambela region in Ethiopia. These groups advocate for changes in inheritance systems within a broader reform agenda by focusing on family laws and land rights (Benschop, 2002; Hill, 2011; Human Rights Watch, 2003; Jutting and Morrisson, 2005; UN, 2010; UN Habitat, 2006; UN Millennium Project, 2005). They conceptualize land inheritance as a way in which the negative socioeconomic impact of the aforementioned adversities on vulnerable individuals or households can be either prevented or exacerbated (Aliber and Walker, 2004; Chapoto et al., 2007; Errico, 2021; Rose, 2006; Strickland, 2004; UN, 2004; UN Women, 2011; World Bank, 2004).

Undoubtedly, the negative socioeconomic effects of denied access to land inheritance impact not only the girl child but her offspring, including her male children, especially when these girls end up as uneducated single mothers due to unfavorable life experiences. In a number of patriarchal societies in SSA, it is commonly expected that, upon marriage, a woman should sever any material claims and benefits (including acquiring and access to land) from her natal family and henceforth be affiliated with her husband's family and, in turn, access land and other material assets through that affiliation. This expectation is extended to the girl child upon coming of age, whether single or unmarried with children. But such expectation only creates false hope that marriage is a woman's salvation and absolves natal family members of responsibility and guilt when the reality is that most married women are never fully accepted as full and permanent members of their husband's clan. The findings from a government study in Kenya presented in a report to the Committee on Economic, Social and Cultural Rights clearly spell out the precarious situation that an African girl child finds herself in: "under the customary law of most ethnic groups in Kenya, a woman cannot inherit land and must live in the land as a guest of male relatives by blood or marriage" (GoK, 2006). A similar study in Tanzania arrived at the same conclusion that family and clan land is customarily inheritable by men, with women acquiring their interests in land through their husbands, especially under the patrilineal system, which is practiced in around 80 percent of Tanzania's ethnic groups (Dancer, 2017).

Scholars have conducted studies to document issues related to land inheritance but largely focusing on the marriage channel; very few have looked exclusively at inheritance via a person's birthright. The inheritance (birthright) channel is mentioned in passing in some of these studies. For example, Doss et al. (2012) examined the relationship between inheritance, marriage, and asset ownership using data on individual-level asset ownership and women's life histories regarding assets in three Ugandan districts (Kapchorwa, Kibale, and Luwero). They found that men who owned land were more likely to have inherited it compared to women. In addition, women, relative to men, were less likely to have the right to sell, bequeath, or rent out land they owned, regardless of how they acquired it (Rugadya et al., 2004; Slavchevska et al., 2021; Genicot and Hernandez-de-Benito, 2022). Dancer (2017), on the other hand, evaluated the contestation around women's inheritance of land in Africa by looking at the patterns of and reasons for resistance and omissions toward enshrining an equal right to inherit land in succession laws in Tanzania and neighboring countries (Kenya and Uganda). However, the study's main focus was on land inheritance via the marriage channel. It highlighted a 2005 landmark case (*Stephen and Charles* v. *Tanzania*) that was brought by two Tanzanian widows to the United Nations Committee on the Elimination of Discrimination against Women in 2012 after being struck down by the Tanzania high court, which cited a codified customary law that outlined the rules of inheritance. In this particular example, the Tanzanian high court used discriminatory customary rules to trump the constitutional rights and international human rights of the two widows.

A related study whose main thesis is on land inheritance via the marriage channel uses information gathered from interviews with government and non-government actors, policy analysis, and reviews of the literature to evaluate how inheritance is being addressed in Ghana, Kenya, Mozambique, Rwanda, and Uganda (Cooper, 2012). It attempts to bring to light how inheritance is understood as a public policy in safe-guarding women's inheritance, marriage, customary land governance, and local arbitration in these five countries.

Another study by Agarwal (2003) sheds light on the experiences of women in India. The paper traces the history of women's land rights in India and explores the prospects and constraints linked to women's access to land through the state, the family, and the market. However, the central focus of the paper is the advantages of poor women acquiring and accessing land via the market and working as a group to lease or purchase land using government credit.

3.1.2 The Marriage Channel

As mentioned, marriage is the most encouraged channel through which women can access and, in some ways, own land in SSA and is highly endorsed by the patriarchal land tenure system. Since the inheritance channel is perceived culturally as anti-marriage, women are presented with and steered toward marriage not just as part of their social obligation but out of necessity as well, to improve their current and future economic well-being. Indeed, in most cases, married women enjoy access to their matrimonial land but at the pleasure of their husbands or sons (in the case of widowhood). In some SSA countries, there is evidence showing that the majority of couples (married and consensual unions) own land jointly (Doss et al., 2012; Jacobs and Kes, 2015); however, most of that land was bequeathed to the male partner through inheritance.

The marriage channel is a bit tricky for women because not only is it conditional on marriage and a woman's good standing in the marriage but, equally, it does not significantly improve women's economic and social welfare (Jacobs and Kes, 2015). It also excludes unmarried, single mothers and those women in cohabiting relationships. For example, the evidence shows that, in most cases, women do not have legal rights to their matrimonial land and are not granted management power (Jacobs and Kes, 2015). In the cases of divorce and widowhood, the privileges of continued use and access are not guaranteed either (Bird and Espey, 2010).

A number of studies have shown widows losing land due to eviction and other forms of land-grabbing by their husband's male relatives, leaving most of these women completely destitute (Dancer, 2017; FAO, 2008; Odeny, 2013). For example, a study in Zambia found that more than a third of widows are denied access to family land after their husbands die. This is not unique to Zambia; rather, it is common practice in much of SSA, and it happens even when statutory laws protect women from such vices (Kimani, 2012; Odeny, 2013). Anecdotal evidence from Tanzania, Burundi, Democratic Republic of Congo, Eritrea, Sierra Leone, and Sudan also reveals cases where widows, divorcees, and victims of civil war and other conflicts have been denied access to their matrimonial and family land in the name of abiding to customs and patriarchal rules (Dancer, 2017; FAO, 2008; Odeny, 2013).

In line with international human rights and the Protocol to the African Charter on Human and Peoples Rights on the Rights of Women in Africa (the Maputo Protocol), several countries in SSA (including Kenya, Rwanda, and Uganda) have deliberately made provisions in their constitution to address the precarious conditions that women face while accessing land via the marriage channel. The Ugandan constitution decrees equal land rights for men and women, both during marriage and in the event of its dissolution (Rugadya et al., 2004). There is evidence that such provisions have improved married women's chances of access to and ownership of land in SSA, but gender discrimination still persists after divorce or widowhood. For instance, Torkelsson and Tassew (2008) analyzed the impact of marital status on women's access to property. Similar to Jacobs and Kes (2015) (for Uganda and South Africa) and Doss et al. (2012) (for Uganda), they found that married women had access to the greatest amount of resources, followed by divorced women, widowed women, and women who had never married. Those who were separated had the least amount of resources. However, these findings should be interpreted within the context, as the probability of women accessing and owning land varies within and across countries. Also, it is important to note that access does not automatically imply ownership, and, moreover, ownership does not imply an equal proportion to men.

3.2 Women's Inheritance and Land Rights: Obstacles

Regardless of their marital status and the channel through which they access or acquire land, women face a myriad of obstacles in their fight to attain gender equality in land rights. A few select obstacles broadly categorized under education and awareness, sociological and cultural, and legal are discussed in what follows.

3.2.1 Obstacles Linked to Education and Awareness

One of the issues that has often posed a challenge to women in their fight for equitable rights to inherit land, especially when government policies accord them such rights, is the lack of education about and awareness of these rights (Massay, 2020; Odeny, 2013). In many instances, African governments have enacted legislative provisions and other legal measures to accommodate women's grievances in accessing, acquiring, and owning land, usually as a response to external pressure. In this regard, they rarely take the additional and necessary step to educate the public about these provisions, especially those people living in rural communities who stand to benefit most from such provisions, the local government officials who are bestowed with the powers to enforce these provisions, and community and clan leaders who are directly responsible for allocating land and addressing land disputes. In the 2017 African Union (AU) report, member states recognized this gap and in fact took the necessary steps through the joint Land Policy Initiative (LPI) by the AU, Economic Commission for Africa (ECA), and African Development Bank (AfDB) to develop training modules on gender mainstreaming in land governance and ensure gender is mainstreamed in the guidelines for curricula development and land governance in Africa and the monitoring and evaluation framework for land governance (AU, 2017). Nongovernmental organizations (NGOs) and other international advocacy groups have also taken on the responsibility not only for advocacy and activism but also for spreading community awareness of women's right to land (see Nandasen, 2012; Tripp, 2004). For example, these organizations and advocacy groups set up legal education centers such as legal aid centers and provide community-based paralegals as well as conducting awareness-raising campaigns that provide behavioral-change tools, especially in cases where women have been conditioned to believe that it is "God-intended" for only men to inherit and own land (Kelkar, 2014).

Land laws that grant women the right to own land can only be effective if there is awareness of these laws, the ability to invoke them, and a general governance environment – and to the extent that statutory laws are practiced instead of cultural norms and traditions (Odeny, 2013).

3.2.2 Sociological and Cultural Obstacles

In many African countries, pluralism in land tenure, which includes customary, religious, and statutory laws, is the norm. Such tenure pluralism complicates women's right to access and own land (Dolcerocca, 2022; Evans, 2016; Genicot and Hernandez-de-Benito, 2022; Lentz, 2007; Meinzen-Dick and Pradhan, 2002), and in most cases the system with the most gender bias prevails (Dancer, 2017; Genicot and Hernandez-de-Benito, 2022; Joireman, 2008).

Resistance to women's access to and ownership of land is deeply embedded in customs and traditions that promote the perception that land symbolizes male dominance, which is necessary for family, community, and clan survival (Agarwal, 1994; Allendorf, 2007; Carney, 1998; Djurfeldt, 2020; Whitehead and Tsikata, 2003). This is more so in patriarchal land tenure systems, whose laws persist even in the presence of statutory laws (Djurfeldt, 2020; Genicot and Hernandez-de-Benito, 2022). Furthermore, despite the efforts that NGOs and advocacy groups have made in educating the public on women's rights to land,

and the penetration of non-customary tenure ideology and legislation, customary tenure not only persists but also, in many SSA countries, is the dominant tenure system (Alden Wily, 2001, Djurfeldt, 2020). For example, the 1996 Cameroon Constitution contains a clause on land that stipulates that every person, regardless of gender, has equal rights to access and control land (Government of Cameroon, 1996). This clause made the Cameroonian land tenure system gender-neutral. However, women in Cameroon often face discrimination in access to and owner-ship of land because, unofficially, the customary norms hold supreme to the legal ordinance (Fonjong et al., 2013; Njieassam, 2019). These customs and traditions, despite being illegal in the eyes of the law, also prevent women from inheriting land.

Nonetheless, women have made and continue to make concerted efforts to counter these sociological and cultural barriers to access, acquire, and own land. Notable examples are the 1995 Beijing Conference (Federici, 2011) and the 2016 Kilimanjaro Initiative that resulted in a land rights charter of demands (Action Aid, 2016). Other activism has resulted in the passing of land acts in several countries (McAuslan, 2013; Odeny, 2013).

The AU recognizes the importance of inclusive land policies in reducing land-related conflicts and therefore has advocated for member states to adopt innovative hybrid approaches that combine the best in community and statutory land systems by drawing from community experiences in order to buttress customary land rights while, at the same time, ensuring that the rights of women and other marginalized groups are respected. In addition to ensuring compatibility between customary and constitutional and statutory safeguards for women's land rights, the AU recommended that member states incorporate gender-responsive provisions in the statutory framework recognizing customary law and that customary law and practices should not be seen to be violating constitutional provisions that protect women's land rights (AU 2017).

3.2.3 Legal Obstacles

There is no doubt that a land tenure system that supports gender equality will empower women by increasing their agricultural production and disposable income and will foster healthy social relationships, among other things (Doss et al., 2012; Odeny, 2013). However, such a system must also grant women the absolute right to own land by issuing title deeds and other legal documents that clearly spell out ownership, with special attention given to communally held land (Errico, 2021). Also, the process must be inexpensive, not conditional on the consent of a male relative, and less complicated, bearing in mind that those with the greatest need tend to be illiterate and poor.

The land titling process via the inheritance channel starts with village elders who allocate land to the rightful heirs. It then moves to government land boards that evaluate the necessary paperwork and make recommendations for title issuance. The problem with both stages is twofold. First, members who serve on the village committees are reluctant to allocate land to women because of strongly held patriarchal beliefs and adherence to customary laws that tend to be discriminatory along gender lines (Genicot and Hernandez-de-Benito, 2022, Errico, 2021). Second, the process is time-consuming, complex, and very expensive, especially for women who are already burdened with care responsibilities (Young, 2010). In many ways, it has deterrence and exclusion mechanisms, especially for poor and illiterate women (Lemke and Claeys, 2020).

The option of land ownership and titling via marriage is even more complex compared to land ownership via inheritance (Jacobs and Kes, 2015). For example, many land boards across SSA do not allocate land to married women without the written consent of their spouses, while the same is not required for married men (Jacobs and Kes, 2015). In other instances, land boards have been reluctant to allocate land to married women on the grounds that it would encourage unruly behavior and break up families (Jacobs and Kes, 2015).

Some authors (Djurfeldt, 2020; Errico, 2021; Lastarria-Cornhiel, 1997) caution about the negative impact of land titling and the formalization of land as it is used to exclude women from land access and ownership. In particular, since the title defines primary legal ownership, some men still use customs and traditions to cheat women in supporting a man as a sole holder and legal bearer of the title deed on the account that he is the head of the family (Fonjong et al., 2013). This, in many cases, also applies to parcels of land purchased or even inherited by women. Moreover, once the man has the title deed, it becomes easier to sell off the land without the consent of his wife or family, leaving women in very precarious economic and social conditions. Thus, the AU-AfDB-ECA Consortium recommended that if law and policy in member countries are to redress gender imbalances in land holding and use, it is necessary to deconstruct, reconstruct, and reconceptualize existing rules of property in land under both customary and statutory law in ways that strengthen women's access to and control of land while respecting family and other social networks (AUC-AfDB-ECA Consortium, 2010).

4 Stylized Facts

Worldwide, women of reproductive age are more likely to live in poverty compared to men, at a ratio of 1.2 to 1 (African Renewal, 2012; Boudet et al., 2018). The gender differential in poverty risk persists into old age, where older

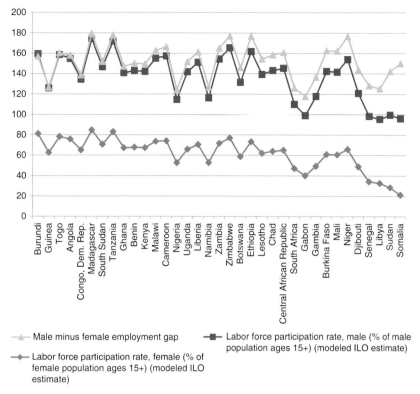

Figure 1 Gender labor force participation rate for selected African countries, averaged over the years 2000–2020

Data source: Author's calculations based on the World Bank's World Development Indicators online database, downloaded on March 20, 2021.

women (aged sixty-five plus) are at a higher risk relative to men in the same age group (UN, 2015). Also, women relative to men are less likely to participate in paid labor (see Table 2 and Figure 1), are less likely to be employers (see Figure 4), tend to be excluded from most economic decision-making within their own households (see Table 4), and are more likely to be excluded from participation in public decision- and policymaking. Further, in more than 50 percent of developing countries (especially in SSA), discriminatory customary laws determine inheritance rights for women and men (UN, 2015; Wekwete, 2013; World Bank, 2012).

By all measures, women in SSA perform relatively poor according to most economic and social indicators (World Bank, 2012). For example, compared to men, they are more likely to be less educated (Table 2), get married early (Table 6), become victims of rape, suffer from sexually transmitted diseases

(including HIV, with the accompanying social stigmatization), be disproportionately impacted by pandemics such as COVID-19, and lack access to banking services and financial credit (Table 6). They are also more likely to be
disproportionately employed in low-wage, low-productivity areas such as
unpaid care work, the informal sector, the services sector, and as contributing
family workers (see Table 3 and Figure 3; African Renewal, 2012; Doss 2006;
Doss et al., 2011; Ellis et al., 2006; Ellis et al., 2007; FAO, 2008; Odeny, 2013;
Wamboye and Seguino, 2015; Wamboye et al., 2015a, 2015b). Compared to
men, they own less than 1 percent of land (FAO, 2011) and are relatively more
impacted by food insecurity and higher food prices (FAO, 2008; Odeny, 2013).
Yet, despite these disadvantages, women are responsible for roughly 70–80
percent of agricultural food production in Africa, comprise 50 percent of farm
labor and 80–90 percent of the workforce in food processing, storage, and
transportation (FAO, 2008; Kimani, 2012), and are the bedrock in molding
the next generation and caring for the elderly and the sick in African countries,
especially in rural communities.

The unfortunate position of women relative to men in SSA is exacerbated by
the fact that the majority (especially those in need) do not own productive
resources such as land, and the infrastructure necessary to increase their productivity and lessen their care burden is either missing or underdeveloped in poor
countries and communities (Wamboye and Seguino, 2015).

4.1 Labor Market Outcomes

The global gender labor force participation gap (measured as the male minus
female labor force participation rate) is estimated at 26.1 percent, with the
female participation rate averaging at 45.3 percent compared to 71.4 percent
for men (ILO, 2019). Comparisons across regions show that, surprisingly, the
participation gap is much lower in SSA (17.8 percent)[4] relative to the Americas
(19.8 percent), Asia and Pacific (31.1 percent), and the Arab States (57.3 percent) (ILO, 2019). But data on the evolution of the participation gap over time
paints a grim picture, indicating that the change has been very slow. For
instance, the Americas' gap narrowed by only 8.9 percentage points from
28.7 to 19.8 percent over the period 1991–2018, while in SSA it reduced by
4.7 percentage points from 22.5 in 1991 to 17.8 percent in 2018. For the Arab
States and the Asia-Pacific region, the change was much smaller. For example,
it changed from 57.6 to 57.3 percent in the former, and 29.9 to 31.1 in the latter
(ILO, 2019). This suggests that the labor force participation gap for the Arab

---

[4] However, this gap must be interpreted within context, where the formal sector in SSA is much
smaller in comparison to other regions.

Table 3 Summary statistics of vulnerable employment (% of total employment) (modeled ILO estimate) segregated by gender

Time	Middle East and North Africa (MENA)			Sub-Saharan Africa (SSA)			World		
	Female	Male	Total	Female	Male	Total	Female	Male	Total
2001	36.60	29.10	30.48	86.32	73.71	79.52	52.25	51.85	52.01
2002	35.75	29.66	30.76	86.56	73.80	79.67	52.01	51.66	51.80
2003	38.41	29.35	31.04	86.44	73.66	79.55	51.79	51.48	51.60
2004	40.32	29.23	31.32	86.00	73.16	79.08	51.35	50.90	51.08
2005	39.84	28.56	30.71	85.93	72.93	78.93	50.81	50.33	50.52
2006	38.92	27.43	29.62	85.64	72.65	78.64	50.09	49.62	49.81
2007	39.72	27.27	29.68	85.14	72.17	78.16	49.47	48.90	49.13
2008	36.86	26.15	28.15	84.46	71.67	77.59	48.91	48.41	48.61
2009	36.69	25.63	27.70	84.47	71.71	77.60	48.71	48.30	48.46
2010	35.18	24.74	26.67	84.00	71.04	77.02	48.22	47.83	47.98
2011	33.65	24.81	26.44	83.22	70.10	76.16	47.51	47.15	47.29
2012	31.84	24.34	25.72	82.72	69.49	75.59	46.68	46.40	46.51
2013	32.04	25.01	26.30	82.39	69.10	75.22	46.26	46.01	46.10
2014	31.27	24.66	25.87	81.87	68.63	74.72	45.76	45.60	45.66
2015	30.32	24.66	25.71	81.65	68.46	74.54	45.35	45.12	45.21
2016	26.68	24.19	24.67	81.35	68.21	74.27	44.97	44.79	44.86

Table 3 (cont.)

Time	Middle East and North Africa (MENA)			Sub-Saharan Africa (SSA)			World		
	Female	Male	Total	Female	Male	Total	Female	Male	Total
2017	27.00	24.52	24.99	80.83	67.75	73.80	44.66	44.42	44.52
2018	25.82	24.27	24.65	80.29	67.41	73.37	44.29	43.95	44.09
2019	24.92	24.54	24.69	80.03	67.18	73.14	43.93	43.65	43.76
Average	33.78	26.22	27.64	83.65	70.67	76.66	48.05	47.70	47.84

Data source: Author's calculations based on the World Bank's World Development Indicators online database, downloaded on March 20, 2021.

States decreased by only 0.3 percentage points and that of the Asia-Pacific increased by 1.2 percentage points.

Across countries within SSA, the labor force participation rate and gender labor force participation gap – as well as the employment rate and gender employment gap – vary remarkably. Figures 1 and 2 provide summary statistics on labor force participation rate and employment rate, respectively. In all countries, with the exception of Burundi, the male labor force participation rate is higher than that of women; and in the majority (57 percent) of the countries, the gender participation gap is more than 10 percentage points (see Figure 1). In fact, in countries such as Burkina Faso, Mali, Niger, Djibouti, Senegal, Libya, Sudan, and Somalia, the male minus female labor force participation gap is more than 20 percent, with Sudan and Somalia having a gap of 43 percent and 54 percent, respectively. The gendered labor force participation rate scenario is replicated in the actual employment numbers, where 54 percent of the countries have a male minus female employment gap of more than 10 percent (Figure 2). Countries such as Gambia, Mali, Djibouti, Gabon, Burkina Faso, Niger, Libya, Senegal, Sudan, and Somalia have a gender employment gap above 20 percent, with Sudan and Somalia employing only 21 percent and 19 percent of the female labor force, respectively, compared to the employment rate of 62 percent (Sudan) and 66 percent (Somalia) for men.

African countries tend to have a dual economy divided into the formal and informal sectors. A larger percentage of these countries' economy is in the informal sector, which accounts for roughly 50–80 percent of the economy, 60–80 percent of employment, and up to 90 percent of new jobs created (AfDB, 2018). This leaves the formal sector comprising as little as 20 percent of the economy, and in many SSA countries the majority of women's production and labor market activities tend to be in the informal sector (African Renewal, 2012; Doss 2006; Doss et al., 2011; Ellis et al. 2006; Ellis et al., 2007; FAO, 2008; Odeny, 2013; Wamboye and Seguino, 2015).

Table 3 provides the annual percentages of vulnerable employment in SSA, the MENA region and worldwide, disaggregated by gender between 2001 and 2019. The ILO defines vulnerable employment as contributing family workers and own-account workers as a percentage of total employment. In reality, this group of workers work within the informal sector and usually earn (if any) below living wages. While a large percentage of employment in SSA tends to be in the vulnerable employment category (which is roughly 77 percent compared to 28 percent in MENA and 48 percent worldwide), women tend to disproportionately fall under this category regardless of the region. For example, between 2001 and 2019, about 84 percent of women employed in SSA were in the vulnerable employment category compared to 71 percent of men employed.

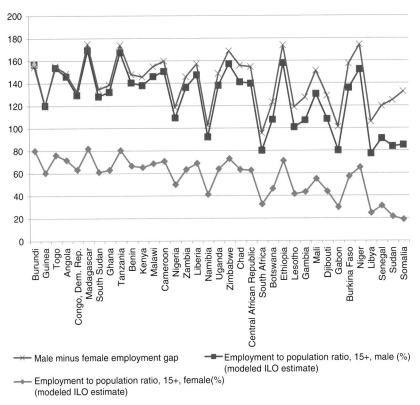

Figure 2 Gender employment rate for selected African countries, averaged over the years 2000–2020

Data source: Author's calculations based on the World Bank's World Development Indicators online database, downloaded on March 20, 2021.

This was true in the MENA region and worldwide, where 34 percent and 48 percent of women employed, respectively, were categorized as being in vulnerable employment, compared to 28 percent and 48 percent of men in the MENA region and worldwide, respectively (Table 3).

In addition to the gendered labor force and employment rates, sectoral employment is also divided along gender lines, with women working predominantly in low-wage, low-productivity agricultural and services sectors while men dominate the high-productivity industrial sector. The evidence in Figure 3 confirms that, indeed, women tend to be disproportionately employed in agriculture, followed by the services sector. For example, between 2000 and 2020, approximately 54 percent and 37 percent of female employment was in the agricultural and services sectors, respectively – compared to 51 percent of men in agriculture and 33 percent in the services sector. While, in general, the

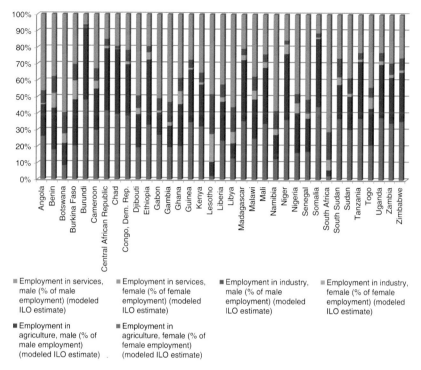

Figure 3 Sector employment in selected African countries disaggregated by gender, averaged over the years 2000–2020

Data source: Author's calculations based on the World Bank's World Development Indicators online database, downloaded on March 20, 2021.

industrial sector tends to contribute less to employment in SSA compared to the agricultural and services sectors, the proportion of women employed in this sector is nearly 50 percent less than that of men. For instance, only 8 percent of female employment was in the industrial sector relative to 16 percent of male employment during the 2000–2020 period. Country-level sectoral distributions of employment vary by gender as well (see Figure 3), but overall, the agricultural sector is the largest employer in SSA countries, followed by the services sector, and lastly, the industrial sector. In fact, the percentage share of employment in industry is in the single digits in most of the countries sampled in Figure 3, for both female and male employment.

Another important dimension for evaluating women's disadvantaged position in the labor market is to compare the percentage of employers by gender. Being an employer signals capital and asset ownership as well as the ability to obtain credit from formal financial institutions. Figure 4 provides the average

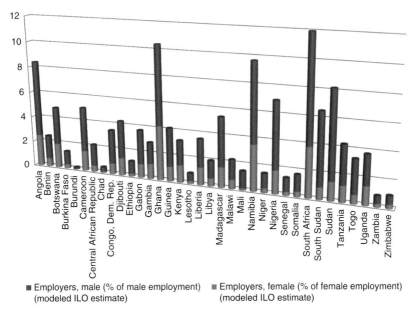

Figure 4 Employers by gender in selected SSA countries, averaged over the years 2000–2020

Data source: Author's calculations based on the World Bank's World Development Indicators online database, downloaded on March 20, 2021.

percentages of female and male employers in selected SSA countries. On average, about 1.2 percent of the female workforce were employers compared to 2.7 percent of the male workforce. While in the majority of these countries less than 2 percent of the female workforce were employers, more than 2 percent (2.7 percent) of the male workforce were categorized as employers. However, in countries such as Angola (2.5 percent), Ghana (4.2 percent), Namibia (3.6 percent), and South Africa (3.9 percent), more than 2 percent (but less than 4 percent) of women were employers. Conversely, in countries such as Angola, Ghana, Namibia, Nigeria, South Africa, South Sudan, and Sudan, the number of men who were employers was between 5 percent and 6 percent. Note that nearly all of the countries that have a higher proportion of female and male employers are richly endowed with either crude oil or minerals and ores.

4.2 Social Indicators

Disparities in economic indicator outcomes, especially as they pertain to labor market outcomes, usually start with opportunities in the social sector that determine human capital development. Limiting our discussion to indicators for which data is available, it is evident not just in this Element but also in other studies (WEF 2016, 2017, 2018) that women relative to men tend to perform poorly in indicators for human capital development. Aside from being highly vulnerable to sexually transmitted diseases such as HIV and AIDS and dispro-portionately impacted (directly and indirectly as caregivers) by pandemics such as COVID-19, women usually have poor education outcomes. For example, the evidence in Table 2 shows that between 2010 and 2019 more than 20 percent of female students dropped out of primary school, which was two percentage points higher than the SSA average and four percentage points higher than the male average

For the group of students that continue on to and attain post-primary and post-secondary education, evidence of gender disparities is abound with women being disadvantaged. Table 4 provides, among other indicators, summarized data for selected SSA countries on post-primary education attainment by gender. The male/female difference in students who complete lower secondary or obtain a post-secondary diploma is much higher, with the completion gap being more than 50 percent at all levels in favor of men.

4.3 Basic Human Rights

In many developing countries, women have fewer rights compared to men. In most cases, they must get approval from their spouses or male relations to enjoy some of the rights. Data from selected SSA countries summarized in Tables 4 and 5 highlights the inequality between men and women associated with freely enjoying basic human rights. For example, in countries with available data, there is evidence demonstrating the power that men have over women in decisions regarding women's own healthcare, freedom to visit family and relatives, and decisions on major household purchases. Particularly in Mali, Niger, and Senegal, more than 50 percent of women indicated that their husband makes decisions pertaining to their own healthcare, visiting family and rela-tives, and major household purchases (see Table 4). On the contrary, less than 15 percent of women in those countries said that they had the power to make decisions on the aforementioned issues. Even in Burundi, where fewer (19–31 percent) women depended on their husbands regarding decisions on these issues, the percentage of women (9–14 percent) who had power over them was still lower (see Table 4).

Table 5 summarizes data on whether women enjoy the same rights as men in applying for a passport, being the head of the household, choosing where to live, getting a job, obtaining a judgment of divorce, opening a bank account, travel-ing outside the country, traveling outside the home, and remarrying. On the

Table 4 Measures of gender empowerment for selected countries in SSA, averaged over the years 2000–2020

	Burundi	Mali	Niger	Senegal
Decision-maker about a woman's own healthcare: mainly husband (% of women aged 15−49)	27.70	78.20	76.30	71.63
Decision-maker about a woman's own healthcare: mainly wife (% of women aged 15−49)	12.30	7.70	3.50	8.77
Decision-maker about a woman's visits to her family or relatives: mainly husband (% of women aged 15−49)	18.70	70.30	58.10	58.27
Decision-maker about a woman's visits to her family or relatives: mainly wife (% of women aged 15−49)	13.70	14.20	10.00	11.17
Decision-maker about major household purchases: mainly husband (% of women aged 15−49)	30.60	76.90	77.30	62.73
Decision-maker about major household purchases: mainly wife (% of women aged 15−49)	9.00	6.60	3.20	5.37
Educational attainment, at least bachelor's or equivalent, population 25+, male (%) (cumulative)	1.40	3.60	1.62	4.21
Educational attainment, at least bachelor's or equivalent, population 25+, female (%) (cumulative)	0.47	1.00	0.57	1.26
Educational attainment, at least completed lower secondary, population 25+, female (%) (cumulative)	7.09	6.05	5.11	9.01
Educational attainment, at least completed lower secondary, population 25+, male (%) (cumulative)	11.73	14.35	12.70	20.08
Educational attainment, at least completed post-secondary, population 25+, female (%) (cumulative)	1.05	3.55	0.96	2.91
Educational attainment, at least completed post-secondary, population 25+, male (%) (cumulative)	2.29	9.03	2.70	8.91

Data source: Author's calculations based on the World Bank's World Development Indicators online database, downloaded on March 20, 2021

Table 5 Basic human rights for selected SSA countries by gender, averaged over the years 2000–2020 (1 = Yes; 0 = No)

A woman can …	Apply for a passport in the same way as a man	Be head of household in the same way as a man	Choose where to live in the same way as a man	Get a job in the same way as a man	Obtain a judgment of divorce in the same way as a man	Open a bank account in the same way as a man	Travel outside the country in the same way as a man	Travel outside her home in the same way as a man	Has the same rights to remarry as a man
Angola	1	1	1	1	1	1	1	1	1
Benin	0	1	0	1	1	1	1	1	0
Botswana	0	1	1	1	1	1	1	1	1
Burkina Faso	1	1	0	1	1	1	1	1	0
Cameroon	0	0	0	0	1	0	1	1	0
Chad	1	0	0	0	1	0	1	1	0
Democratic Republic of Congo	1	0	0	0	1	0	1	1	0
Ghana	1	1	1	1	1	1	1	1	1
Guinea	1	0	0	0	0	1	1	1	0
Kenya	1	1	1	1	1	1	1	1	1
Lesotho	1	1	1	1	1	1	1	1	1
Malawi	0	1	0	1	1	1	1	1	1
Senegal	1	0	0	1	1	1	1	1	0
South Africa	1	1	1	1	1	1	1	1	1

Table 5 (cont.)

A woman can …	Apply for a passport in the same way as a man	Be head of household in the same way as a man	Choose where to live in the same way as a man	Get a job in the same way as a man	Obtain a judgment of divorce in the same way as a man	Open a bank account in the same way as a man	Travel outside the country in the same way as a man	Travel outside her home in the same way as a man	Has the same rights to remarry as a man
Togo	1	0.5	1	1	1	1	1	1	0
Uganda	0	1	0	1	0	1	1	1	1
Zambia	0	1	0	1	0	1	1	1	1
Zimbabwe	1	1	1	1	0	1	1	1	1
Percentage (Yes)	66.67	69.44	44.44	77.78	77.78	83.33	100.00	100.00	55.56

Data source: Author's calculations based on the World Bank's World Development Indicators online database, downloaded on March 20, 2021.

lower end of the spectrum, where women's rights are infringed, women can choose where to live and enjoy the same rights to remarry in the same way as a man in only 44 percent and 56 percent of SSA countries, respectively. In 67 percent of the countries, women can apply for a passport; and in 69 percent of them, they can be head of a household in the same way as a man. Regarding applying for a job, obtaining a divorce, and opening a bank account in the same way as men, the evidence shows that it is only possible in 78–83 percent of the countries. However, in all the countries for which data is available, woman can travel outside the country and outside the home in the same way as a man. Nevertheless, there should be a cautionary note that in some countries (such as Kenya), while the question of spouse name is not asked of men, women are required to provide their husband's name on the passport application form.

Men are also more likely than women to own an account at a financial institution or with a mobile money-service provider at a ratio of two to one, and in countries such as Benin, Botswana, Cameroon, Chad, Guinea, Lesotho, and Uganda the ratio is a bit higher (see Table 6). Furthermore, girls are more likely to get married at a younger age compared to men. For example, data in Table 6 shows that, on average, women get married at the age of twenty-one, while men marry at about twenty-seven years of age. In fact, in countries such as Chad, Guinea, and Malawi the average age of marriage for girls is less than twenty years; and in countries such as Senegal and South Africa, the average age of marriage for boys is thirty to thirty-one years (Table 6).

4.4 Property Ownership

Table 7 provides data on immovable asset (land and house) ownership by gender for six countries for which comparable data was available. It is important to note here that the data does not provide us with information on how these assets were acquired. As mentioned, men in SSA countries are more likely than women to acquire land and other immovable properties via inheritance from their families, while women do so via purchase or marriage. In addition to information on the percentages of men and women who own or do not own land or house individually, Table 7 also provides data on the percentages of men and women who own land jointly (with their spouse) and on the question of whether men and married women have equal ownership rights to immovable assets.

Focusing on land alone, data indicates that a large percentage of both men and women do not own land in SSA. However, whereas between 57 percent (Democratic Republic of Congo) and 78 percent (Senegal) of men do not own land in SSA, the proportion of women who do not own land is much higher – between 61 percent (Kenya) and 92 percent (Senegal). The proportion of those

Table 6 Basic human rights for selected SSA countries by gender, averaged over the years 2000–2020

	Account ownership at a financial institution or with a mobile money-service provider, male (% of population ages 15+)	Account ownership at a financial institution or with a mobile money-service provider, female (% of population ages 15+)	Age at first marriage, female	Age at first marriage, male
Angola	37.81	22.33	20.70	25.50
Benin	26.51	13.60	21.20	25.80
Botswana	47.87	28.36	24.80	29.80
Burkina Faso	27.69	34.50	20.00	26.40
Cameroon	24.08	10.53	21.75	27.85
Chad	19.32	7.83	18.90	25.40
Democratic Republic of Congo	17.57	14.32	20.90	25.50
Ghana	45.10	33.23	24.15	27.85
Guinea	13.84	4.12	19.80	28.00
Kenya	70.05	71.13	21.90	26.30
Lesotho	32.42	16.87	24.40	28.50
Malawi	25.53	13.98	19.80	24.60
Senegal	24.30	18.43	21.93	30.30
South Africa	65.01	51.02	28.00	31.20
Togo	28.58	26.35	21.80	27.60
Uganda	48.07	15.06	20.00	24.30
Zambia	36.40	33.25	21.80	25.90
Zimbabwe	45.91	44.39	20.85	25.75
Average	35.34	25.52	21.82	27.03

Data source: World Development Indicators online dataset, downloaded on January 30, 2021.

who own land individually is smaller for both men and women, but for women, it is almost negligible. The evidence in Table 7 shows that between 17 percent (Senegal) and 30 percent (Kenya) of men own land, whereas only 3 percent

Table 7 Property ownership by gender for selected countries in SSA, averaged over the years 2000–2020

	Democratic Republic of Congo	Ghana	Kenya	Senegal	Togo	Zambia
Men who do not own a house (% of men)	53.2	73	48.6	75.4	70.3	54.8
Men who do not own land (% of men)	57	64	53.4	78.45	67.8	63.3
Men who own a house alone (% of men)	28.5	21	37.8	13.6	26.9	23.9
Men who own land alone (% of men)	21.8	28.2	30.2	16.65	28.6	19.5
Men who own land jointly (% of men)	17.3	6.8	12.6	4.55	3.2	12.1
Men and married women have equal ownership rights to immovable property (1 = yes; 0 = no)	0	1	1	1	1	1
Women who do not own a house (% of women aged 15–49)	62.7	81.1	57.7	89.55	89.5	53.8
Women who do not own land (% of women aged 15–49)	65.8	78.1	61.3	92.8	90.3	67.1
Women who own a house both alone and jointly (% of women aged 15–49)	5.3	3.8	3.8	1.1	2.1	6.2
Women who own a house jointly (% of women aged 15–49)	25.6	10.8	30.6	8.45	5.7	30.4
Women who own land alone (% of women aged 15–49)	7.6	8.1	7.1	3.35	4.5	6.7
Women who own land both alone and jointly (% of women aged 15–49)	4.7	3.7	3.4	0.8	1.4	4.5
Women who own land jointly (% of women aged 15–49)	21.9	10	28.2	3.05	3.6	21.4

Data source: World Development Indicators online dataset, downloaded on January 30, 2021.

(Senegal) to 8 percent (Ghana) of women own land in SSA. With reference to joint ownership of land, evidence suggests that more women compared to men own land jointly (with their spouse). This could be attributed to the fact that women who own property prior to marriage are more likely to convert to joint ownership compared to men. For example, only around 3 percent (Togo) to 17 percent (Democratic Republic of Congo) of men own land jointly with women; this is compared to 3 percent (Senegal) to 28 percent (Kenya) of women. Another interesting statistic in Table 7 is on the question of whether men and married women had equal ownership rights of immovable assets. In all but one country (Democratic Republic of Congo) listed in Table 7, the response was yes.

Figure 5 provides data for forty-two SSA countries on male and female land ownership but only for 2019. The difference between the percentage of men and women who own land in these countries is about 40 percent, whereby on average 31 percent of women in SSA own land, compared to 69 percent of men. As shown in Figure 5, the difference is consistent across the forty-two countries, suggesting that the constraints that women face in accessing and

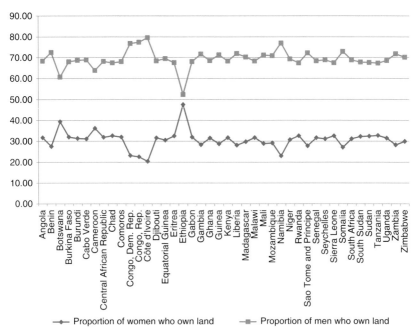

Figure 5 Proportion of men and women who own land in selected SSA countries, 2019

Data source: African Development Bank (AfDB) estimation, 2019.

owning land in these countries are more or less similar. Slavchevska et al. (2021) also arrived at much the same conclusion in their study of six African countries (Ethiopia, Malawi, Niger, Nigeria, Tanzania, and Uganda). In particular, they found that in five (Ethiopia, Niger, Nigeria, Tanzania, and Uganda) of the six countries analyzed, fewer women than men were reported as landowners, with the gap being wider in West African (Niger and Nigeria) countries in the study compared to the East African (Ethiopia, Tanzania, and Uganda) countries. This is also consistent with the data in Figure 5 and Table 7 in this Element.

5 Pairwise Correlation

In an attempt to give a data-driven dimension to the discussion on female ownership of land via inheritance and its consequences on various measures of women's economic and social well-being, we conducted pairwise correlation, which provides an uncontrolled relation between various land ownership measures and proxies for women's economic and social well-being. The results in Table 8 provide the correlation index that signifies the strength as well as direction of relationship and the corresponding standard errors in brackets. Limiting our discussions to the relationships that are statistically significant, we find that lack of land ownership by men is positively and highly correlated with women completing at least lower secondary school (0.85), women getting married early (0.53), and an increase in female unemployment (0.53). On the other hand, male ownership of land is negatively correlated with women's age at first marriage (0.44) and female unemployment (0.57).

There are various deductions that can be drawn from these findings. As mentioned, land is the single most important asset in SSA and a source of wealth and social status in most communities. A man who owns land is able to marry with the assurance that he will be able to feed and take care of his family. Also, because many households depend on family labor to work on family farms, a man relies on his wife (or wives) and children to provide that labor. Thus, in communities where a household places higher value on farm labor relative to education, the children will more likely provide that labor and hence not get an education. Conversely, a man that does not own land could be forced to look for alternative means of acquiring wealth, which could be via either formal or informal employment in urban centers. In such instances, the family could be forced to move to an urban area (usually the country's capital city), where the father is also likely to educate his children either due to agglomeration effects (where other households in the vicinity are educating their children) or because his children's education is a form of investment in his own future social

Table 8 Pairwise correlation matrix for selected gender social and economic indicators in selected SSA countries, 2001–2020

	Do not own land (Men)	Own land alone (men)	Own land jointly (Men)	Do not own land (women)	Own land alone (women)	Own land jointly (women)
Do not own land (women)	0.793	−0.470	−0.692			
	(0.000)	(0.005)	(0.000)			
Own land alone (women)	−0.499	0.538	0.107	−0.613		
	(0.003)	(0.001)	(0.547)	(0.000)		
Own land jointly (women)	−0.696	0.285	0.806	−0.897	0.242	
	(0.000)	(0.102)	(0.000)	(0.000)	(0.155)	
Employers (F)	0.129	0.003	−0.207	0.168	−0.058	−0.271
	(0.462)	(0.98 8)	(0.233)	(0.321)	(0.738)	(0.110)
Employers (M)	0.170	−0.008	−0.244	0.287	−0.097	−0.374
	(0.328)	(0.966)	(0.158)	(0.086)	(0.575)	(0.025)
Education (F)	0.846	−0.502	−0.646	0.432	−0.357	−0.568
	(0.071)	(0.389)	(0.239)	(0.334)	(0.487)	(0.240)
Education (M)	0.589	−0.661	−0.146	0.462	−0.781	−0.329
	(0.21 8)	(0.153)	(0.783)	(0.249)	(0.038)	(0.471)
Dropout (F)	−0.245	0.108	0.412	−0.233	0.468	0.301
	(0.360)	(0.691)	(0.113)	(0.352)	(0.058)	(0.240)

Dropout (M)	−0.128 (0.637)	−0.012 (0.964)	0.343 (0.194)	−0.177 (0.483)	0.343 (0.177)	0.267 (0.300)
Finances (F)	−0.244 (0.497)	0.13 4 (0.713)	0.265 (0.460)	−0.391 (0.264)	0.225 (0.532)	0.437 (0.206)
Finances (M)	−0.285 (0.425)	0.176 (0.626)	0.286 (0.423)	−0.409 (0.240)	0.241 (0.50 3)	0.458 (0.184)
Marriage (F)	0.52 8 (0.002)	−0.436 (0.013)	−0.265 (0.143)	0.152 (0.390)	−0.247 (0.166)	−0.168 (0.350)
Marriage (M)	0.827 (0.000)	−0.650 (0.000)	−0.490 (0.004)	0.729 (0.000)	−0.551 (0.001)	−0.667 (0.000)
Unemployment (F)	0.533 (0.001)	−0.573 (0.000)	−0.037 (0.833)	0.286 (0.086)	−0.125 (0.468)	−0.285 (0.092)
Unemployment (M)	0.566 (0.000)	−0.588 (0.000)	−0.081 (0.6438)	0.314 (0.059)	−0.175 (0.308)	−0.314 (0.063)
	(0.000)	(0.000)				

Note: p-values in parentheses. Description of variable notation is provided in Table A4 in the Appendix.

welfare. But, in the unfortunate situation where the man is unable to find any form of employment or other source of income or income-generating activities, he might turn to his female children as a source of wealth and marry them off early. Lack of land resource could also cause the father to move his family to an urban slum settlement, which might also lead to his female children getting married early due to the poor conditions. Moreover, in such situations, unemployment among women could be higher due to an increase in the supply of uneducated, low-skilled women competing for the same limited job positions.

We observe the opposite in the case where men own land; the likelihood that a woman will be married off at a young age or face unemployment decreases. As discussed, a man with wealth (land resource) is more likely to use his family members as farm labor, thereby reducing female unemployment. Also, because he is not in urgent need of the bride-price due to ownership of land, he is less likely to marry off his female children early. Moreover, by the fact that the female children are kept busy on the farm, they are less likely to think of early marriage.

The results in Table 8 also show a significant and positive relationship between women not owning land and the number of men who are employers (0.29), age of first marriage by men (0.73), and female unemployment (0.29). Furthermore, women owning land alone has a negative correlation with male education (0.78) and is positively correlated with female school dropout (0.47). Land ownership by women provides the same economic and social security enjoyed by men, but the social and economic multiplier effects are more than that of men (Jones and Frick, 2010). In SSA, women are the biggest source of farm labor (as evidenced by their high employment rate in the agricultural sector) and the biggest producers of food crops. They are the primary caregivers for the young and the old and are directly involved in both children's education and their healthcare. They are more likely to be single parents, exacerbating not only their burdens of care but also their economic and social responsibilities. Thus, a woman's ownership of land will lead to an increase in food production to feed her family and for the market since she has a reliable farm where she can grow food crops. Land ownership also implies financial security for the woman, which comes directly via farming and indirectly by being able to use her piece of land as collateral for obtaining loans. On the other end of the spectrum, having land wealth enhances women's social and political standing in the society, where they are able to participate in household decision-making and in political discourse that has a direct impact on a woman's rights and freedoms.

Thus, the results in Table 8 imply that, when women do not own land, they depend on men as employers, since the majority of women tend to be employed in the agricultural sector. This suggests that they will be employed on farms owned by men. Also, lack of land ownership means that women have to find other avenues to provide food for their families, which leads them to seek employment from businesses owned mostly by men. In addition, lack of land ownership by women directly increases unemployment for them, since, as shown, most women tend to be employed in the agricultural sector and tend to be own-account workers.

The most surprising finding is that women's ownership of land leads to a decrease in male education and an increase in female school dropout. Plausible reasons for this could be that families or societies that grant equal rights to land ownership for both men and women (especially via inheritance) are also more likely to grant equal rights to education for both genders. In such instances, fewer resources are available for education due to crowding-out effects as families divide their limited resources toward educating both their male and their female children. In terms of the female school dropout component, it could be explained by the wealth syndrome, where girls who expect to inherit land and other resources from their families find less value in gaining an education in anticipation of the potential lifetime source of income that comes from owning land. This is a common scenario in societies all over the world, where children from wealthy families place less value on education in as far as they perceive it as a means of acquiring future wealth.

6 Regression Analysis

6.1 Methodology

In the empirical model, we investigate the effects of women's ownership of land (*LAND*) on women's absolute employment (*EMP*) in thirty-three SSA countries using cross-sectional data for 2019. We control for other determinants of women's absolute employment, broadly categorized as demand-side shifters (trade measure and share of agricultural and services sectors in GDP) and supply-side shifters (dependency ratio and a measure of HIV prevalence).

Demand-side shifters include structural economic conditions and a country's trade policies that directly or indirectly affect the quantity of labor demanded, as well as cultural and religious norms that are transferable to the labor market. The share of the agricultural (*AGRI*) and services (*SERV*) sectors' output in GDP are used as a measure of structural economic conditions. This is consistent with what has been observed in the preceding narrative, whereby women are more likely to be employed in the agricultural and services sectors compared to the industrial sector. In addition to the share of sectoral output in GDP, we include demand effects arising from global economic integration. Particularly, we include a measure of trade openness proxied by the share of a country's exports in GDP (*EXP*). A better proxy would be a policy variable, such as tariffs or quota, but we do not have sufficient data on these variables. Therefore, we follow what has been used in related literature and resort to the policy outcome measures. While it is expected that trade openness will have favorable effects on women's employment, Heintz (2006) asserts that these effects depend on a country's production structure and development policy management.

Supply-side factors, on the other hand, include those factors that capture both the quality and the quantity of women's absolute labor supplied. An increase in women's labor supply can have crowding-out effects on the available employment opportunities, thereby reducing overall female employment. The age dependency ratio (*DEP*) – the ratio of old dependents to the working-age population (those aged 15–64) – and incidence of HIV on people aged 15–49 (per 1,000 uninfected population aged 15–49) are used as proxies for the female labor supply, specifically capturing the quantity dimension of the labor supply. The age dependency ratio plays a crucial role in determining women's economic activities because, in most societies, women continue to be the primary caregivers for both the old and the young. Therefore, a higher dependency ratio implies that women's time spent in their reproductive roles, relative to formal market production activities, increases (Budlender 2008). We hypothesize that the age dependency ratio and incidences of HIV infections will have negative effects on women's absolute employment. Owing to data constraints, we did not include a measure of the quality of female labor supplied, which in this case would have been proxied by an education outcome. Nonetheless, exclusion does not negatively impact the explanatory power of the model as observed through stepwise regressions and R-square. Following the discussion above, we estimate equation (1) as:

$$EMP_i = \beta_0 + \beta_1 LAND_i + \beta_2 AGRI_i + \beta_3 SERV_i + \beta_4 EXP_i + \beta_5 DEP_i$$
$$+ \beta_6 HIV_i + \varepsilon_i \tag{1}$$

Where ε_i is the standard error term and i denotes the country. The other notations are as previously defined in the preceding paragraphs. It is important to note that the choice of variables, countries used in the study, and model estimation technique was limited by the availability of data. The land ownership data was available only for 2019, which posed a constraint on the sample selection and model specification.

6.2 Data Description

Aside from the data on the percentage of land ownership by women that was obtained from the AfDB, the rest of the data was downloaded from the World Bank's World Development Indicators online database, which was downloaded in March 2021. Descriptive statistics of model variables and the correlation coefficient matrix are reported in the Appendix in Tables A1 and A2, respectively. A list of countries in our sample that was used for regression purposes is given in Table A3.

Table 9 Cross-sectional stepwise OLS regression for female land ownership effects on female employment rate for selected SSA countries

	(1)	(2)
Percentage of women who own land	1.105***	1.132***
	(0.354)	(0.314)
Agriculture, forestry, and fishing, value added (% of GDP)	0.612***	0.724***
	(0.199)	(0.203)
Services, value added (% of GDP)	0.635***	0.475**
	(0.220)	(0.255)
Age dependency ratio, old (% of working-age population)	−3.777*	−4.899*
	(2.120)	(1.791)
Incidence of HIV, ages 15−49 (per 1,000 uninfected population ages 15−49)	0.822	0.392
	(1.189)	(1.026)
Exports of goods and services (% of GDP)		0.400**
		(0.184)
R-square	0.948	0.955
No. of observations	33	33
No. of countries	33	33

Note: Robust standard errors in parenthesis. *** 1 percent level of significance, ** 5 percent level of significance * 10 percent level of significance

6.3 Results Analysis

Table 9 provides the results of stepwise regression using ordinary least squares (OLS) methodology. Overall, there is evidence that an increase in women's ownership of land positively impacts women's employment. For example, a 1 percentage increase in women's ownership of land (regardless of how the land was acquired) leads to an approximately 1.1 percent increase in women's employment prospects at 1 percent level of significance. There are a number of reasons for the positive link between female land ownership and an increase in women's employment, most of which have been discussed in the preceding analysis.

The rest of the control variables have the expected signs, and in fact the effects are significant with the exception of the impact of HIV prevalence. For example, an increase in the share of the agricultural and services sectors' output in GDP by 10 percentage points increases female employment by 6–7 percent and 5–6 percent, respectively, across SSA countries (Wamboye et al., 2015a, 2015b; Wamboye and Seguino, 2015). Equally an increase in export value added in GDP by 10 percent increases female employment by 4 percent. Conversely, an increase in women's burden of care as proxied by a dependency ratio of older people by 1 percentage point negatively impacts women's participation in the formal labor market by 4–5 percentage points.

7 Conclusion and Policy Recommendations

7.1 Conclusion

In 2009, the African heads of state and government signed the AU Declaration on Land to ensure equitable land access for all land users and to improve access of land tenure for women (AU, 2017). Later, in 2010, the cross-national governing bodies in Africa – the AU, the AfDB and the ECA – jointly published a White Paper on framework and guidelines on land policy in Africa. It acknowledged that discrimination against female ownership and control of land and its resources still exists in Africa and is perpetuated by the patriarchal system that dominates Africa's social structures (AUC-ECA-AfDB Consortium, 2010). This system, which is enshrined in imported land laws instituted during the colonial period, has been reinforced by conferring titles and inheritance rights upon male family members on the assumption that women and girls can access land through their male relations (AUC-ECA-AfDB Consortium, 2010). In principle, the system of patriarchy ensures that women at no stage in their natural life can claim land ownership beyond enjoying access privileges through their male relations or through purchase from the market system.

Furthermore, the AU-ECA-AfDB Consortium cited the "claw-back" clauses that exist in many African constitutions and are used to allow gender discrimination in land inheritance on matters of personal law, which often operate against women's right to equal treatment on land access, ownership, and inheritance. This is despite the fact that African states have made commitments to the rights of women in Africa as evidenced not only in the 2009 AU Declaration but also in the AU's 2003 Maputo Protocol to the African Charter on Human and Peoples' Rights (ACHPR) and the 2004 Solemn Declaration on Gender Equality in Africa, which call for actions to address gender inequalities, including women's unequal access to land (AUC-ECA-AfDB Consortium, 2010).

In 2017, the AU published a Declaration on Land Issues and Challenges in Africa, outlining its key commitments on Land Governance in its Agenda 2063, which included gender equality (AU Goal 17) and a commitment to the UN SDG 5 on "undertaking reforms to give women equal rights to economic resources, as well as access to ownership and control over land and other forms of property, financial services, inheritance and natural resources, in accordance with national laws" (SDG 5, Target 5a). To achieve AU Goal 17 and SDG 5, the AU's implementation plan recommended that member states commit to ensuring 20 percent of rural women in their respective countries have access to and control of land by 2023. In the same implementation plan, the AU recommended that, by 2030, all men and the poor, in particular the poor and the vulnerable, have equal rights of ownership and control over land (AU, 2017).

Another study in 2015 on "Land, Ethnicity and Conflict in Africa" was conducted by the AU-ECA-AfDB's Land Policy Initiative (LPI). The findings and resulting recommendations from that research were published in an AU report in 2017 (AU, 2017). One of the key recommendations was that member states allocate 30 percent of documented land rights to women and improve the land rights of women through legislative or other mechanisms. The findings also resulted in the development of training modules on gender mainstreaming in land governance and ensuring gender is mainstreamed in the guidelines for curricula development and land governance in Africa and monitoring and evaluation framework for land governance (AU, 2017). As a way to provide sustained support to achieve the 30 percent target, a Gender, Women and Land Program has been included as part of the African Land Policy Centre (ALPC) to coordinate the implementation of commitments relating to women and land.

Despite all these efforts, there is a big gap between AU recommendations, national statutes on the books in member countries, and implementation, particularly as pertaining to women's rights to inherit and own land (Doss et al., 2012). To date, the plural land tenure system still persists in nearly all SSA countries, with a customary tenure system most often prevailing in cases of female land inheritance. As shown in the preceding analysis, women in SSA currently own 40 percentage points less land compared to men; and a large proportion of the land owned by women is usually acquired through either marriage or purchase. In fact, in the entire developing world, women hold only 1–2 percent of all titled land (Rabenhorst, 2011). This is contrary to the evidence showing multiplier effects of women's economic empowerment through asset ownership on the economic and social welfare of families and of countries (Arekapudi and Almodóvar-Reteguis, 2020; Jones and Frick, 2010; Rabenhorst, 2011). The opposite is true with male economic empowerment, as men tend to spend their additional wealth on their personal welfare rather than that of their family (Rabenhorst, 2011).

According to the recent World Bank World Development Indicators data (2000–2020), women form about 50–52 percent of SSA's population. More than 50 percent of the female labor force in the region is employed in the agricultural sector; and in some countries such as Tanzania, more than 80 percent of female labor is in agriculture. Women are the biggest producers of food crops, accounting for approximately 70–80 percent of agricultural food production in Africa and 80–90 percent of the workforce in food processing, storage, and transportation (FAO, 2008; Kimani, 2012). In African countries, they are also the bedrock in molding the next generation and caring for the elderly and the sick, especially in rural communities. And, as shown in this Element, there is a direct and significant link between female land ownership and women's absolute employment. Other cross-country studies have also found that gender-based inequalities cost countries about 15 percent of GDP (Cuberes and Teignier, 2016; Ferrant and Kolev, 2016).

How does one reconcile the established and overwhelming evidence of the beneficial effects of female land ownership and the reluctance of countries in SSA to establish and or proactively enforce national laws that accord women the same rights as men to inherit land? The famous African saying that "land belongs to the man and the produce [*food*] in it to the woman" embodies the struggle that women face in their quest to own and inherit land in SSA (Arekapudi and Almodóvar-Reteguis, 2020). Data from the recent World Bank publication on women, business and the law reveals that two-fifths of countries worldwide limit women's property rights; in nineteen countries women do not have equal ownership rights to immovable property; and in forty-four countries, male and female surviving spouses do not have equal rights to inherit assets (Arekapudi and Almodóvar-Reteguis, 2020). Unfortunately, reforms related to property ownership and inheritance are the most difficult to pass, especially in SSA, where the patriarchal land tenure system dictates how land is acquired and passed on to future generations (Arekapudi and Almodovar-Reteguis, 2020). Undoubtedly, the plight of women in poverty will continue unless there is significant reform and strengthening of laws, policies, and practices relating to ownership and control of property (Rabenhorst, 2011; Slavchevska et al., 2021). Improving the property rights of women is both a human right and a means to achieve gender equality, as well as a fundamental principle that underlies economic development in SSA (Rabenhorst, 2011).

Of equal importance is the channel though which women should acquire and own land and other immovable property. As mentioned, the channel through which societies in SSA prefer women to access and own land, especially in patrilineal societies, is through marriage or purchase from the market system. However, both channels subject women to conditions that men in the same capacity are not subject to. Moreover, unmarried and separated women are by default excluded from this channel. The second channel is conditional on women having sufficient wealth to purchase land from the market system. Even in some parts of SSA, women cannot purchase land without their husband's consent (the case of Cameroon, see Ngwa, 2012 for). The inheritance channel, which male (relative to female) children are freely entitled to by virtue of their gender, comes with no constraints and has very minimal costs (related to obtaining a title deed). It also comes with a sense of belonging and a feeling of being wanted. Thus, acquiring land through the inheritance channel ensures that women can live with agency and dignity (Arekapudi and Almodóvar-Reteguis, 2020) and are not subject to the pressures and ills that come with marriage.

7.2 Policy Implications

The ALPC – a joint program of the tripartite consortium consisting of the African Union Commission (AUC), the AfDB, and the ECA – was formed in 2015 to provide leadership and coordination, build partnerships, and promote land policy advocacy in African countries as well as assist them in developing or reviewing their land policies and implementing and evaluating these policies. Prior to the ALPC, African countries had already embarked on a process of reviewing and assessing their land sectors and formulating new land policies for reform but without any real guidance from experienced experts and without a comprehensive plan that considered all stakeholders, data, and the development needs of the countries (AUC-ECA-AfDB Consortium, 2010). Thus, the ALPC provides a continent-wide vision as well as guidance and support to subregions and individual countries. Nevertheless, progress has been made in the last three decades, with many of these countries actively addressing land issues through processes of policy reform and implementation (AUC-ECA-AfDB Consortium, 2010, 2011).

The question of Africa's land policy and land reform is as old as the continent itself – starting with the arrival of European settlers who took control of large swathes of Africa's fertile land (through conquest, appropriation, and "99-year agreements") to postcolonial reforms and modern-day pro-development and pro–human rights reforms. In countries or places where these settlers had direct control of land, Indigenous people were pushed out of their ancestral lands and into townships (South Africa) or reservations (Kenya) and denied ownership. These new spaces were often congested and left African men feeling emasculated due to their inability to protect their land and provide for their families. To cement their control and ownership of acquired lands, the settlers promulgated a variety of laws across African countries, often informed by imported European laws and packaged to fit a diverse range of Indigenous economic and cultural practices (AUC-ECA-AfDB Consortium, 2010). The result was a dualistic land tenure system that still governs land policy in many African countries today (AUC-ECA-AfDB Consortium, 2010).

The imported land laws were most often gender-biased and it is not surprising that many African governments are hesitant to meaningfully change these laws to fit the changing economic, political, and social landscape; and in cases, where they have managed to change them, and especially embraced gender equality in land inheritance, implementation has been slow or mute to the new laws as far as men feel their position in the status quo has been infringed on.

The reality is that many African countries already have laws on the books that support equal rights to land inheritance, whether via marriage or birthright. The biggest problem is implementing or enforcing these laws. There are a number of obstacles that need to be addressed in land policies in order for the new land policies to be effective and, in turn, benefit men and women equally.

7.2.1 Customs and Traditions Are Dynamic, Not Static

Resistance to women's access to and ownership of land is deeply embedded in static customs and traditions that promote the perception that land symbolizes male dominance, which is necessary for family, community, and clan survival (Agarwal, 1994; Allendorf, 2007; Carney, 1998; Whitehead and Tsikata, 2003). However, it is now well understood that customs and traditions are not static; they evolve and respond to the changing social, economic, and political climate. Customs and traditions that tend to remain static are those that benefit one group at the expense of another, and they persist when the benefiting group controls the economic, political, and social spheres of a community or nation.

The AU recognizes the importance of inclusive land policies in reducing land related conflicts and therefore has advocated that "Member States adopt innovative hybrid approaches that combine the best in community and statutory land systems by drawing from community experiences in order to buttress customary land rights while, at the same time, ensuring that the rights of women and other marginalized groups are respected." In addition to ensuring compatibility between customary and constitutional and statutory safeguards for women's land rights, the AU recommended that "Member States incorporate gender responsive provisions in the statutory framework recognizing customary law and that customary law and practices should not be seen to be violating constitutional provisions that protect women's land rights" (AU 2017).

7.2.2 Economic Development and Household Welfare

Land is an important economic resource, a cornerstone of economic development, and a means of achieving food security and overcoming extreme poverty in Africa. From an entrepreneurial perspective, land plays a vital role in investment strategies. In order to access financial credit via the formal financial sector, land title is required (in most countries in SSA) as a major collateral. Beyond the economic relevance, land ownership in SSA is a source of social identity and political power, cultural heritage, and insurance for the continuity of the clan/family lineage.

Therefore, in devising effective and gender-sensitive land policies, African governments should approach it from the perspective of enhancing household welfare and overall economic development rather than from cultural and social lenses. In as far as land ownership improves women's economic, social, and political welfare, it is more likely to strengthen rather than weaken the institution of marriage (by providing women secure positions in the marriage and also increasing overall household assets and wealth); improve human capital development through improved healthcare access, household nutrition, and children's education; and increase food security and reduce hunger since women in Africa are the biggest contributors to food production.

7.2.3 Education and Awareness of the Land Rights

Land laws that grant women the right to own land can only be effective if there is awareness of these laws, the ability to invoke them, and a general governance environment – and to the extent that statutory laws are practiced instead of cultural norms and traditions (Odeny, 2013). In this regard, African governments that have already instituted gender-sensitive land policies should take a proactive role to increase awareness and educate the public, especially all the stakeholders involved in upholding these land rights and the women that stand to benefit from these rights. Moreover, those governments that are in the process of designing these policies should incorporate the education and awareness component in their implementation packages to ensure that these policies are effective and produce the intended outcome.

7.2.4 Land Titling, Legal Complexities, and Cost

A land tenure system that supports gender equality will empower women by increasing their agricultural production and disposable income and will foster healthy social relationships as well. However, such a system must also grant women the primary right to own land by issuing title deeds and other legal documents that clearly spell out ownership (Errico, 2021). Also, the process must be inexpensive and less complicated, bearing in mind that those with the greatest need tend to be illiterate and poor.

Consequently, African governments should aim to simplify the titling process, staff land boards with people who are well educated in the laws regarding land rights, and the village committees should be gender-balanced with members purposefully elected by the community. Moreover, the village committee members should be objective and tasked with upholding the principles of equal rights to property ownership and should be well trained in matters concerning land rights. The government should also require that, upon marriage, couples should convert individually owned land to joint ownership, with titles reflecting equal and joint ownership. Laws regarding the sale of joint property should be clearly spelled out, and property division during separation or divorce should be clearly outlined and well understood by the enforcing government agents. The government should also have laws protecting vulnerable women to avoid their being preyed on by cunning husbands or male relatives. The African Union Consortium also recommends that member countries deconstruct, reconstruct, and reconceptualize existing rules of property in land under both customary and statutory law in ways that strengthen women's access to and control of land while respecting family and other social networks (AUC-AfDB-ECA, 2010).

Appendix

Table A1 Summary statistics for variables used in the regression analysis

	Mean	Std. Deviation	Minimum	Maximum	Obs
Percentage of Women who own land	57.664	15.614	20.900	83.030	33
Agriculture, forestry, and fishing, value added (% of GDP)	20.891	13.267	1.880	54.340	33
Services, value added (% of GDP)	45.696	9.750	12.810	61.390	33
Age dependency ratio, old (% of working-age population)	5.379	0.961	3.810	8.250	33
Exports of goods and services (% of GDP)	28.414	14.347	7.673	69.088	33
Incidence of HIV, ages 15–49 (per 1,000 uninfected population ages 15–49)	2.049	2.559	0.010	8.940	33

Table A2 Correlation-coefficient matrix for regression variables

	(1)	(2)	(3)	(4)	(5)	(6)	(7)
Employment to population ratio, 15+, female (%) (modeled ILO estimate) (1)	1.000						
Percentage of Women who own land (2)	0.127	1.000					
Agriculture, forestry, and fishing, value added (% of GDP) (3)	0.369	0.142	1.000				
Services, value added (% of GDP) (4)	0.050	−0.045	−0.334	1.000			
Age dependency ratio, old (% of working-age population) (5)	−0.414	0.156	−0.219	0.160	1.000		
Exports of goods and services (% of GDP) (4)	−0.056	−0.363	−0.560	0.227	0.033	1.000	
Incidence of HIV, ages 15–49 (per 1,000 uninfected population ages 15–49) (7)	−0.031	−0.031	−0.457	0.353	0.123	0.391	1.000

Table A3 List of countries used in the regression analysis

Angola	Congo, Rep.	Malawi
Benin	Cote d'Ivoire	Mozambique
Botswana	Equatorial Guinea	Namibia
Burkina Faso	Ethiopia	Niger
Burundi	Gabon	Rwanda
Cabo Verde	Gambia	Senegal
Cameroon	Ghana	Sierra Leone
Central African Republic	Guinea	South Africa
Chad	Kenya	Sudan
Comoros	Liberia	Uganda
Democratic Republic of Congo	Madagascar	Zambia

Table A4 Variable notation definitions

Do not own land (men)	Men who do not own land (% of men)
Own land alone (men)	Men who own land alone (% of men)
Own land jointly (men)	Men who own land jointly (% of men)
Do not own land (women)	Women who do not own land (% of women age 15−49)
Own land alone (women)	Women who own land alone (% of women age 15−49)
Own land jointly (women)	Women who own land jointly (% of women age 15−49)
Employers (F)	Employers, female (% of female employment) (modeled ILO estimate)
Employers (M)	Employers, male (% of male employment) (modeled ILO estimate)
Education (F)	Educational attainment, at least completed lower secondary, population 25+, female (%) (cumulative)
Education (M)	Educational attainment, at least completed lower secondary, population 25+, male (%) (cumulative)
Dropout (F)	Children out of school, primary, female
Dropout (M)	Children out of school, primary, male
Finances (F)	Account ownership at a financial institution or with a mobile money-service provider, female (% of population ages 15+)

Table A4 (cont.)

Finances(M)	Account ownership at a financial institution or with a mobile money-service provider, male (% of population ages 15+)
Marriage (F)	Mean age at first marriage, female
Marriage (M)	Mean age at first marriage, male
Unemployed (F)	Unemployment, female (% of female labor force) (modeled ILO estimate)
Unemployed (M)	Unemployment, male (% of male labor force) (modeled ILO estimate)

References

Acemoglu, D., and Robinson, J. A. (2012). *Why Nations Fail: The Origins of Power, Prosperity, and Poverty*. New York: Crown Publishing.

Action Aid. (2016). *Charter of Demands: Actualizing Women's Land Rights in Africa*. Arusha: Kilimanjaro Initiative. https://actionaid.org/publications/2017/charter-demands-actualizing-womens-land-rights-africa.

AfDB (African Development Bank). (2018). *Africa Economic Outlook 2018*. Abidjan: African Development Bank Group. www.afdb.org/fileadmin/uploads/afdb/Documents/Publications/African_Economic_Outlook_2018_-_EN.pdf.

Afridi, F. (2010). "Women's Empowerment and the Goal of Parity between the Sexes in Schooling in India." *Population Studies*, 64(2): 131–145.

Agarwal, B. (1994). *A Field of One's Own: Gender and Land Rights in South Asia*. Cambridge: Cambridge University Press.

Agarwal, B. (1997). "'Bargaining' and Gender Relations: Within and beyond the Household." *Feminist Economics*, 3(1): 1–51.

Agarwal, B. (2003). "Gender and Land Rights Revisited: Exploring New Prospects via the State, Family and Market." *Journal of Agrarian Change*, 3(1–2): 184–224.

Aldasher, G., Chaara, I., Platteau, J.-P., and Wakhaj, Z. (2012). "Using the Law to Change the Custom." *Journal of Development Economics*, 97: 182–200.

Alden Wily, L. (2001). "Reconstructing the African Commons." *Africa Today*, 48(1): 77–99.

Aliber, M. and Walker, C. (2004). *The Impact of HIV/AIDS on Land Rights: Case Studies from Kenya*. Cape Town: Human Sciences Research Council.

Allendorf, K. (2007). "Do Women's Land Rights Promote Empowerment and Child Health in Nepal?" *World Development*, 35(11): 1975–1988.

Arekapudi, N. and Almodóvar-Reteguis, N. L. (2020). "Women's Property Rights Are the Key to Economic Development." World Bank Blogs, February 24. https://blogs.worldbank.org/developmenttalk/womens-property-rights-are-key-economic-development.

AU (African Union). (2017). *AU Declaration on Land Issues and Challenges: A Review of Progress Made*, October. https://au.int/sites/default/files/documents/33005-doc-draft_report_to_au_stc_progress_in_implementing_the_au_declaration_on_land_issues_and_challenges_in_africa_2017_revised_with_guideline.pdf.

AUC (African Union Commission). (2011). *Promoting Employment for Social Cohesion and Inclusive Growth*. Addis Ababa: AUC.

AUC-ECA-AfDB Consortium. (2010). *Framework and Guidelines on Land Policy in Africa*. Addis Ababa: African Union, African Development Bank, and Economic Commission for Africa. www.un.org/en/land-natural-resources-conflict/pdfs/35-EN-%20Land%20Policy%20Report_ENG%20181010pdf.pdf.

AUC-ECA-AfDB Consortium. (2011). *Land Policy in Africa: A Framework to Strengthen Land Rights, Enhance Productivity and Secure Livelihoods*. Addis Ababa: African Union, African Development Bank, and Economic Commission for Africa.

Benjamin, N. and Mbaye, A. (2012). *The Informal Sector in Francophone Africa*. Paris and Washington, DC: Agence Française de Dévelopment and The World Bank.

Benschop, M. (2002). *Rights and Reality: Are Women's Equal Rights to Land, Housing and Property Implemented in East Africa?* Nairobi: United Nations Centre for Human Settlements.

Berge, E., Kambewa, D., Munthali, A., and Wiig, H. (2014). "Lineage and Land Reforms in Malawi: Do Matrilineal and Patrilineal Landholding Systems Represent a Problem for Land Reforms in Malawi." *Land Use Policy*, 41: 61–69.

Bhatla, N., Chakraborty, S., and Duvvury, N. (2006). *Property Ownership and Inheritance Rights of Women As Social Protection from Domestic Violence: Cross-Site Analysis*. Washington, DC: International Center for Research on Women. www.icrw.org/wp-content/uploads/2016/10/Property-Ownership-and-Inheritance-Rights-of-Women-for-Social-Protection-The-South-Asia-Experience.pdf.

Bird, K. (2007). "The Intergenerational Transmission of Poverty: An Overview." Chronic Poverty Research Centre Working Paper No. 99. http://dx.doi.org/10.2139/ssrn.1629262.

Bird, K. and Espey, J. (2010). "Power, Patriarchy and Land: Examining Women's Land Rights in Uganda and Rwanda. In S. Chant (ed.), *International Handbook on Gender and Poverty: Concepts, Research, Policy*. Cheltenham: Edward Elgar, 360–366.

Bose, N. and Das, S. (2017). "Women's Inheritance Rights, Household Allocation, and Gender Bias." *American Economic Review: Papers and Proceedings*, 107(5): 150–153.

Boudet, A. M., Buitrago, P., Leroy de la Briere, B., et al. (2018). "Gender Differences in Poverty and Household Composition through the Life-cycle." World Bank Group Policy Research Working Paper No. 8360.

Budlender, D. (2008). "The Statistical Evidence on Care and Non-care Work across Six Countries." United Nations Research Institute for Social Development (UNRISD) Gender Programme Paper No. 4.

Budlender, D. and Alma, E. (2011). *Women and Land: Securing Rights for Better Lives*. Ottawa, ON: International Development Research Centre.

Carney, J. A. (1998). "Women's Land Rights in Gambian Irrigated Rice Schemes: Constraints and Opportunities. *Agriculture and Human Values*, 15: 325–336.

Chapoto, A., Jayne, T., and Mason, N. (2007). "Security of Widows' Access to Land in the Era of HIV/AIDS: Panel Survey Evidence from Zambia." Food Security Research Project Working Paper No. 19.

Claassens, A. and Ngubane, S. (2008). "Women, Land and Power: The Impact of the Communal Land Rights Act." In A. Claassens and B. Cousins (eds.), *Land, Power and Custom: Controversies Generated by South Africa's Communal Land Rights Act*. Cape Town: UCT Press, 154–183.

Cooper, E. (2012). "Women and Inheritance in Sub-Saharan Africa: What Can Change?" *Development Policy Review*, 30(5): 641–657.

Cooper, E. and Bird, K. (2012). "Inheritance: A Gendered and Intergenerational Dimension of Poverty." *Development Policy Review*, 30(5): 527–541.

Cuberes, D. and Teignier, M. (2016). "Aggregate Effects of Gender Gaps in the Labor Market: A Quantitative Estimate." *Journal of Human Capital*, 10(1): 1–32.

Dancer, H. (2017). "An Equal Right to Inherit? Women's Land Rights, Customary Law and Constitutional Reform in Tanzania." *Social and Legal Studies*, 26(3): 291–310.

Deere, C. D. (2017). "Women's Land Rights, Rural Social Movements, and the State in the 21st-Century Latin American Agrarian Reforms." *Journal of Agrarian Change*, 17(2): 258–278.

Deere, C. D. and Doss, C. R. (2006). "Gender and the Distribution of Wealth in Developing Countries." United Nations University World Institute for Development Economics Research (WIDER) Research Paper No. 2006/115.

Deere, C. D. and León, M. (2009). *Empowering Women: Land and Property Rights in Latin America*. Pittsburg, PA: University of Pittsburgh Press.

Deere, C. D., Oduro, A. D., Swaminathan, H., and Doss, C. (2013). "Property Rights and the Gender Distribution of Wealth in Ecuador, Ghana and India." *The Journal of Economic Inequality*, 11: 249–265.

DESA (Department of Economic and Social Affairs). (2022). "LDCs at a Glance." United Nations DESA (web page). www.un.org/development/desa/dpad/least-developed-country-category/ldcs-at-a-glance.html.

Djurfeldt, A. A. (2020). "Gendered Land Rights, Legal Reform and Social Norms in the Context of Land Fragmentation: A Review of the Literature for Kenya, Rwanda and Uganda." *Land Use Policy*, 90(1): 1–10.

Dolcerocca, A. (2022). "State Property vs. Customary Ownership: A Comparative Framework in West Africa." *The Journal of Peasant Studies*, 49(5): 1064–1078. https://doi.org/10.1080/03066150.2021.1907353.

Doss, C. R. (2006). "The Effects of Intrahousehold Property Ownership on Expenditure Patterns in Ghana." *Journal of African Economies*, 15(1): 149–180.

Doss, C., Deere, C. D., Oduro, A. D., et al. (2011). *The Gender Asset and Wealth Gaps: Evidence from Ecuador, Ghana, and Karnataka, India*. Bangalore: Indian Institute of Management Bangalore.

Doss, C., Truong, M., Nabanoga, G., and Namaalwa, J. (2012). "Women, Marriage and Asset Inheritance in Uganda." *Development Policy Review*, 30(5): 597–616.

Duflo, E. (2003). "Grandmothers and Granddaughters: Old-Age Pensions and Intrahousehold Allocation in South Africa." *The World Bank Economic Review*, 17(1): 1–25.

ECA (United Nations Economic Commission for Africa). (2015). *Economic Report on Africa: Harnessing the Potential of the Informal Sector for Inclusive Growth in Africa*. Addis Ababa: ECA. www.un.org/en/ecosoc/integration/2015/pdf/eca.pdf.

Ellis, A., Blackden, M., Cutura, J., MacCulloch, F., and Seebens, H. (2007). *Gender and Economic Growth in Tanzania: Creating Opportunities for Women*. Washington, DC: The World Bank.

Ellis, A., Manuel, C., and Blackden, C. M. (2006). *Gender and Economic Growth in Uganda: Unleashing the Power of Women*. Washington, DC: The World Bank.

Ellis, F. and Mdoe, N. (2003). "Livelihoods and Rural Poverty Reduction in Tanzania." *World Development*, 31(8): 1367–1384.

Errico, S. (2021). "Women's Right to Land between Collective and Individual Dimensions." *Frontiers in Sustainable Food Systems*, 5: 690321.

Evans, R. (2015). "HIV-Related Stigma, Asset Inheritance and Chronic Poverty: Vulnerability and Resilience of Widows and Caregiving Children and Youth in Tanzania and Uganda." *Progress in Development Studies* 15(4): 326–342.

Evans, R. (2016). "Gendered Struggles Over Land: Shifting Inheritance Practices among the Serer in Rural Senegal." *Gender, Place & Culture*, 23(9): 1360–1375.

Evans, R., Mariwah, S., and Barima Antwi, K. (2015). "Struggles over Family Land? Tree Crops, Land and Labour in Ghana's Brong-Ahafo Region." *Geoforum* 67: 24–35.

FAO (Food and Agriculture Organization of the United Nations). (2008). *Land Reform: Land Settlement and Cooperatives*. Rome: FAO. www.fao.org/3/i0470t/i0470t.pdf.

FAO (Food and Agriculture Organization of the United Nations). (2011). *The State of Food and Agriculture 2010–2011. Women in Agriculture: Closing the Gender Gap for Development*. Rome: FAO. www.fao.org/3/i2050e/i2050e.pdf.

Federici, S. (2011). "Women, Land Struggles, and the Reconstruction of the Commons." *Journal of Labor and Society*, 14(1): 41–56.

Ferrant, G. and Kolev, A. (2016). "Does Gender Discrimination in Social Institutions Matter for Long-Term Growth? Cross-Country Evidence." Organisation for Economic Co-operation and Development (OECD) Development Centre Working Paper No. 330.

Ferrara, E. La and Milazzo, A. (2017). "Customary Norms, Inheritance, and Human Capital: Evidence from a Reform of the Matrilineal System in Ghana." *American Economic Journal: Applied Economics*, 9(4): 166–185.

Fonjong L., Fombe, L., and Sama-Lang, I. (2013). "The Paradox of Gender Discrimination in Land Ownership and Women's Contribution to Poverty Reduction in Anglophone Cameroon." *GeoJournal*, 78(3): 575–589.

Genicot, G. and Hernandez-de-Benito, M. (2022). "Women's Land Rights and Village Institutions in Tanzania." *World Development*, 153: 105811.

Global Fund for Women. (2018). "Top Ten Moments for Women's Rights in 2018," December 13 (web page). www.globalfundforwomen.org/top-ten-moments-womens-rights-2018/.

GoK (Government of Kenya). (2006). *Initial Report of States Parties to the Committee on Economic, Social and Cultural Rights*. U.N. Doc. E/C.12/KEN/1. September 7.

Government of Cameroon. (1996). *Constitution of the Republic of Cameroon*. Yaounde: National Printing Press.

Grynberg, R. (2013). "Some Like Them Rough: The Future of Diamond Beneficiation in Botswana." European Centre for Development Policy Management Discussion Paper No. 142.

Heintz, J. (2006). "Globalization, Economic Policy and Employment: Poverty and Gender Implications." ILO Employment Strategy Paper No. 2006/3.

Hill, C. (2011). "Enabling Rural Women's Economic Empowerment: Institutions, Opportunities, and Participation." Background Paper for Expert Group Meeting, Accra, September 20–23.

Human Rights Watch. (2003). *Double Standards: Women's Property Rights Violations in Kenya*. New York: Human Rights Watch.

Hunt, J. and Kasynathan, N. (2001). "Pathways to Empowerment? Reflections on Microfinance and Transformation in Gender Relations in South Asia." *Gender & Development*, 9(1): 42–52.

ILO (International Labour Organization). (2019). *World Employment Social Outlook – Trends 2019*. Geneva: ILO.www.ilo.org/global/research/global-reports/weso/2019/lang–en/index.htm.

Izumi, K. (2007). "Gender-Based Violence and Property Grabbing in Africa: A Denial of Women's Liberty and Security."*Gender and Development*, 15(1): 11–23.

Jacobs, K. and Kes, A. (2015). "The Ambiguity of Joint Asset Ownership: Customary Tales from Uganda and South Africa." *Feminist Economics*, 21(3): 23–55.

Joireman, S. F. (2007). "Enforcing New Property Rights in Sub-Saharan Africa: The Ugandan Constitution and the 1998 Land Act." *Comparative Politics*, 39(4): 463–480.

Joireman, S. F. (2008). "The Mystery of Capital Formation in Sub-Saharan Africa: Women, Property Rights and Customary Law." *World Development*, 36(7): 1233–1246.

Jones, A. S. and Frick, K. D. (2010). "The Roles of Women's Health and Education in Family and Societal Health'. *Women's Health Issues*, 20(4): 231–233.

Jütting, J. and Morrisson, C. (2005). *Changing Social Institutions to Improve the Status of Women in Developing Countries*. Policy Brief 27. Paris: Organisation for Economic Co-operation and Development (OECD).

Kabeer, N. (2001). "Conflicts Over Credit: Re-evaluating the Empowerment Potential of Loans to Women in Rural Bangladesh." *World Development*, 29(1): 63–84.

Kalabamu, F. (1998). "Effects of Gendered Land Rights on Urban Housing by Women in Botswana." Paper presented at the Proceedings of the International Conference on Land Tenure in the Developing World with a Focus on Southern Africa. University of Cape Town, Cape Town, January.

Kalabamu, F. (2006). "Patriarchy and Women Land Rights in Botswana." *Land Use Policy*, 23(3): 237–246.

Katz, E. and Chamorro, J. S. (2003). "Gender, Land Rights, and the Household Economy in Rural Nicaragua and Honduras." Paper presented at the Annual Conference of the Latin American and Caribbean Economics Association, Puebla, Mexico, October.

Kelkar, G. (2014). "The Fog of Entitlement: Women's Inheritance and Land Rights." *Economic and Political Weekly*, 49(33): 51–58.

Kimani, M. (2012). "Women Struggle to Secure Land Rights: Hard Fight for Access and Decision-Making Power." *Africa Renewal* [UN Magazine]. www .ilo.org/global/research/global-reports/weso/2019/lang–en/index.htm.

Kumar, N., Quisumbing, A. R. (2012). "'Beyond Death Do Us Part': The Long-Term Implications of Divorce Perceptions on Women's Well-Being and Child Schooling in Rural Ethiopia." *World Development*, 40(12): 2478–2489.

Lambert, S., Ravallion, M., and van de walle, D. (2014). "Intergenerational Mobility and Interpersonal Inequality in an African Economy." *Journal of Development Economics*, 110: 327–344.

Lastarria-Cornhiel, S. (1997). "Impact of Privatization on Gender and Property Rights in Africa." *World Development*, 25(8): 1317–1333.

Lemke, S. and Claeys, P. (2020). "Absent Voices: Women and Youth in Communal Land Governance: Reflections on Methods and Process from Exploratory Research in West and East Africa." *Land*, 9(266). https://doi .org/10.3390/Land9080266.

Lentz, C. (2007). "Land and the Politics of Belonging in Africa." In P. Chabal, U. Engel, and L. de Haan (eds.), *African Alternatives*. Leiden: Brill, 37–54.

MacInnes, J. (1998). *The End of Masculinity*. Buckingham: Open University Press.

Massay, G. (2020). "The Struggles for Land Rights by Rural Women in Sub-Saharan Africa: The Case of Tanzania." *African Journal of Economic and Management Studies*, 11(2): 271–283.

McAuslan, P. (2013). *Land Law Reform in Eastern Africa: Traditional or Transformative? A Critical Review of 50 Years of Land Law Reform in Eastern Africa 1961–2011*. New York: Routledge.

Meinzen-Dick, R. S. and Pradhan, R. (2002). "Legal Pluralism and Dynamic Property Rights." International Food Policy Research Institute CAPRi Working Papers No. 22.

Meinzen-Dick, R. S., Quisumbing, A., Doss, C., and Theis, S. (2019). "Women's Land Rights As a Pathway to Poverty Reduction: Framework and Review of Available Evidence." *Agricultural Systems*, 172: 72–82.

Molapo, E. (1994). "Women and Patriarchy in Lesotho: A Deconstructive Study." Doctoral thesis, University of Free State Bloemfontein. https:// scholar.ufs.ac.za/bitstream/handle/11660/7608/MolapoELM.pdf? sequence=1&isAllowed=y.

Mujere, J. (2014). "Land, Gender and Inheritance Disputes among the Basotho in the Dewure Purchase Areas, Colonial Zimbabwe." *South African Historical Journal*, 66(4): 699–716.

Nandasen, N. (2012). "Rural Women's Access to Land in Sub-Saharan Africa and Implications for Meeting the Millennium Development Goals." *Agenda*, 26(1): 41–53.

Ngwa, N. E. (2012). "Introduction to Land and Rural Women in Cameroon." In L. N. Fonjong (ed.), *Issues on Women's Land Rights in Cameroon*. Oxford: African Books Collective. http://dx.doi.org/10.17159/1727-3781/2019/v22i0a4907.

Njieassam, E. E. (2019). "Gender Inequality and Land Rights: The Situation of Indigenous Women in Cameroon."*Potchefstroom Electronic Law Journal*, 22: 1–33. http://dx.doi.org/10.17159/1727-3781/2019/v22i0a4907.

Odeny, M. (2013). "Improving Access to Land and Strengthening Women's Land Rights in Africa." Paper presented at the Annual World Bank Conference on Land and Poverty, May 2017; Addis Ababa. Accessed from https://hdl.handle.net/10855/24140.

Odgaard, R. (2002). "Scrambling for Land in Tanzania: Processes of Formalisation and Legitimisation of Land Rights." *The European Journal of Development Research*, 14(2): 71–88.

Peterman, A. (2012). "Widowhood and Asset Inheritance in Sub-Saharan Africa: Empirical Evidence from 15 Countries." *Development Policy Review*, 30(5): 543–571.

Quisumbing, A. R. and Maluccio, J. A. "Resources at Marriage and Intrahousehold Allocation: Evidence from Bangladesh, Ethiopia, Indonesia, and South Africa." *Oxford Bulletin of Economics and Statistics*, 65(3): 283–327.

Rabenhorst, C. S. (2011). *Gender and Property Rights: A Critical Issue in Urban Economic Development*. New York: The International Housing Coalition and the Urban Institute. www.urban.org/sites/default/files/publication/27491/412387-Gender-and-Property-Rights.PDF.

Rose, L. (2006). *Children's Property and Inheritance Rights and their Livelihoods: The Context of HIV and AIDS in Southern and East Africa*. Rome: Food and Agriculture Organization.

Rugadya, M. (2010). Women's Land Rights in Uganda: Status of Implementation of Policy and Law on Women's Land Rights for ECA, ACGS Addis Ababa. 2010. Working Paper, Academia.edu. Accessed from https://www.academia.edu/43052736/Status_of_Implementation_of_Policy_and_Law_on_Womens_Land_Rights_for_ECA_ACGS_Addis_Ababa

Rugadya, M., Nsamba, E., Lule, R. et al. (2008). *Final Report of the Integrated Study on Land and Family Justice*. Kampala: Ministry of Justice and Constitutional Affairs.

Rugadya, M., Obaiko, E., and Kamusiime, H. (2004). *Gender and the Land Reform Process in Uganda: Assessing Gains and Losses for Women in Uganda*. Land Research Series No. 2. Kampala: Associates for Development.

Saiget, M. (2016). "(De-)Politicising Women's Collective Action: International Actors and Land Inheritance in Post-war Burundi." *Review of African Political Economy*, 43(149): 365–381.

Santos, F., Fletschner, D., and Daconto, G. (2014). "Enhancing Inclusiveness of Rwanda's Land Tenure Regularization Program: Insights from Early Stages of its Implementation." *World Development*, 62: 30–41.

Santpoort, R., Steel, G., Mkandawire, A. et al. (2021). "The Land Is Ours: Bottom-Up Strategies to Secure Rural Women's Access, Control and Rights to Land in Kenya, Mozambique, Senegal and Malawi." *Frontiers in Sustainable Food Systems*, 5. https://doi.org/10.3389/fsufs.2021.697314.

Sen, A. (1999). *Development As Freedom*. New York: Anchor Books.

Slavchevska, V., Doss, C. R., de la O Campos, A. P, and Brunelli, C. (2021). "Beyond Ownership: Women's and Men's Land Rights in Sub-Saharan Africa." *Oxford Development Studies*, 49(1): 2–22. https://doi.org/10.1080/13600818.2020.1818714.

Strickland, R. (2004). *To Have and To Hold: Women's Property and Inheritance Rights in the Context of HIV/AIDS in Sub-Saharan Africa*. Washington, DC: International Center for Research on Women.

Swaminathan, H., Walker, C., and Rugadya, M. A. (eds). (2008). *Women's Property Rights, HIV and AIDS and Domestic Violence: Research Findings from Two Districts in South Africa and Uganda*. Cape Town: HSRC Press.

Torkelsson, Å. and Tassew, B. (2008). "Quantifying Women's and Men's Rural Resource Portfolios: Empirical Evidence from Western Shoa in Ethiopia." *European Journal of Development Research*, 20: 462–481.

Tripp, A. (2004). "Women's Movements, Customary Law, and Land Rights in Africa: The Case of Uganda." *African Studies Quarterly*, 7(4): 1–19.

UN (United Nations). (2004). *Property and Inheritance Rights and HIV/AIDS: Women and Girls in Southern Africa*. New York: UN Secretary General's Task Force on Women, Girls and HIV/AIDS in Southern Africa.

UN (United Nations). (2010). "'Keeping the promise': United to achieve the Millennium Development Goals." Resolution adopted by the UN General Assembly 65th Session, 19 October.

UN (United Nations). (2015). *The World's Women 2015: Trends and Statistics*. New York: UN Department of Economic and Social Affairs. https://unstats.un.org/unsd/gender/downloads/worldswomen2015_report.pdf.

UN (United Nations). (2018). "LDCs at a glance" (web page). UN Department of Economic and Social Affairs. www.un.org/development/desa/dpad/least-developed-country-category/ldcs-at-a-glance.html.

UN-Habitat. (2006). *Progress Report on Removing Discrimination Against Women in Respect of Property and Inheritance Rights*. Nairobi: United Nations Centre for Human Settlements.

UN Millennium Project. (2005). *Taking Action: Achieving Gender Equality and Empowering Women*. Report by the Task Force on Education and Gender Equality. New York: UN Millennium Project.

UN Women. (2011). "UN Women awards nearly $1.5 million in small grants towards realizing women's property and inheritance rights in the context of HIV/AIDS." UN Women News (web page), March 14. www.unwomen.org/en/news/stories/2011/3/un-women-awards-nearly-1-5-million-in-small-grants-towards-realizing-women-s-property-and-inheritan.

UN Women. (2018). "Securing Rural Women's Access to Land in Cameroon." UN Women Africa News, October 22. https://africa.unwomen.org/en/news-and-events/stories/2018/10/access-to-land.

UN Women. (2022). "Poverty deepens for women and girls, according to latest projections." Women Count Data Hub (web page), February 1. https://data.unwomen.org/features/poverty-deepens-women-and-girls-according-latest-projections.

Walker, C. (2005). "Women, Gender Policy and Land Reform in South Africa." *Politikon*, 32(2): 297–315.

Wamboye, E. F., Adekola, A., and Sergi, B, S. (2015a). "Sectoral Shifts and Women's Employment: A Study of Thirty-Nine Least Developed Countries'. *Journal of Economic Issues*, 49(4): 1045–1076.

Wamboye, E. F., Adekola, A., and Sergi, B, S. (2015b). "Sectoral Effects of Female Absolute and Relative Employment in Selected Least Developed Countries." *Gender, Technology and Development*, 19(1): 1–42.

Wamboye, E. F. and Seguino, S. (2015). "Gender Effects of Trade Openness in Sub-Saharan Africa." *Feminist Economics*, 21(3): 82–113.

Wanyeki, L. M. (2012). "African Women's Long Walk to Freedom." *Africa Renewal*. www.un.org/africarenewal/magazine/special-edition-women-2012/african-women%E2%80%99s-long-walk-freedom.

WEF (World Economic Forum). (2016). *The Global Gender Gap Report 2016*. Geneva: World Economic Forum. www3.weforum.org/docs/GGGR16/WEF_Global_Gender_Gap_Report_2016.pdf.

WEF (World Economic Forum). (2017). *The Global Gender Gap Report 2017*. Geneva: World Economic Forum. www3.weforum.org/docs/WEF_GGGR_2017.pdf.

WEF (World Economic Forum). (2018). *The Global Gender Gap Report 2016*. Geneva: World Economic Forum. www3.weforum.org/docs/WEF_GGGR_2018.pdf.

Wekwete, N. N. (2013). "Gender and Economic Empowerment in Africa: Evidence and Policy." *Journal of African Economies*, 23 (AERC Suppl. 1): i87–i127.

Whitehead, A. and Tsikata, D. (2003). "Policy Discourses on Women's Land Rights in Sub-Saharan Africa: The Implications of the Return to the Customary." *Journal of Agrarian Change*, 3(1–2): 67–112.

World Bank (2004). *Integrating Gender into HIV/AIDS Programs: An Operational Guide*. Washington, DC: World Bank.

World Bank. (2012). *World Development Report 2012: Gender Equality and Development*. Washington, DC: World Bank.

Yeboah, E. (2014). "Women's Land Rights and Africa's Development Conundrum: Which Way Forward." International Institute for Environment and Development (IIED) (blog), December 12. www.iied.org/womens-land-rights-africas-development-conundrum-which-way-forward.

Young, D. (2010). "The Jurisprudence of Vulnerability: Property Rights, Domestic Violence and HIV/AIDS Among Women in Uganda." *International Review of Constitutionalism*, 9(2): 327–360.

Cambridge Elements ☰

Economics of Emerging Markets

Bruno S. Sergi

Harvard University

Editor Bruno S. Sergi is an Instructor at Harvard University, an Associate of the Harvard University Davis Center for Russian and Eurasian Studies and Harvard Ukrainian Research Institute. He is the Academic Series Editor of the Cambridge *Elements in the Economics of Emerging Markets* (Cambridge University Press), a co-editor of the *Lab for Entrepreneurship and Development* book series, and associate editor of *The American Economist*. Concurrently, he teaches International Economics at the University of Messina, Scientific Director of the Lab for Entrepreneurship and Development (LEAD), and a co-founder and Scientific Director of the International Center for Emerging Markets Research at RUDN University in Moscow. He has published over 150 articles in professional journals and twenty-one books as author, co-author, editor, and co-editor.

About the Series

The aim of this Elements series is to deliver state-of-the-art, comprehensive coverage of the knowledge developed to date, including the dynamics and prospects of these economies, focusing on emerging markets' economics, finance, banking, technology advances, trade, demographic challenges, and their economic relations with the rest of the world, as well as the causal factors and limits of economic policy in these markets.

Cambridge Elements $\equiv$

Economics of Emerging Markets

Printed in the United States
by Baker & Taylor Publisher Services